As We Walk
Through the Valley

As We Walk Through The Valley

A True Story of Love, Loss, and Hope

AMY CONNER

authorHOUSE®

AuthorHouse™
1663 Liberty Drive
Bloomington, IN 47403
www.authorhouse.com
Phone: 1-800-839-8640

First published by AuthorHouse   09/28/2011

ISBN: 978-1-4567-9763-8 (sc)
ISBN: 978-1-4567-9762-1 (ebk)

Library of Congress Control Number: 2011915371

Printed in the United States of America

Dedication

I dedicate this book to my angels on Earth, Mckenna and Luke — and to our angel in Heaven, their Daddy.

CONTENTS

Preface

What is it about life that causes us to break our pattern of "everyday" living and try, instead, to find the true meaning *behind* it? Is it one of those earth shattering moments, like learning you have cancer or suffering a massive heart attack, that knocks you off of your center and sends you scrambling back to your feet? Is it something subtle, like a quote or a saying, that catches your attention and makes you think? Is it a significant welcoming of a beautiful new life, or is it the devastating loss of a loved one of whom you were not ready to let go?

Everyone has a story, and this is mine. The unbelievable devastating loss of a loved one of whom I was not ready to let go. Of all the valuable lessons that I have learned from this loss, one has held true to me more than anything else. There is not a person out there who has not experienced loss. In losing someone, it does not make you an expert on someone else's pain. There were very few people who could look into my heart-broken, terrified eyes and understand the depth of my pain. So in turn, I do not pretend that I understand another's pain. I am an expert on my life and my loss only.

Empathy. Compassion. Love. Patience. Presence. Support. These are just a few characteristics from the people in my life that I did cling to. I clung to these with all of my heart and soul, because in those dark days, it was all I felt I had. And through the help of these people, I was able to scrape myself up off of the ground and begin to trust in truly living again. This is a scary thing to do when you realize that we live in a world filled with such uncertainties. There are no guarantees. The only thing we are guaranteed is that the time we spend with these loved ones is a gift to us from above. We are not even guaranteed a chance to say goodbye.

This is what I was left *without* . . . the chance to say goodbye. What do you do with this? What do you hold in your hands when you are left with nothing to hold? How do you say goodbye when there is nobody there to say it to? How do you pick up all of the pieces knowing that they are mere crumbles of what should have been? How do you look forward to the day ahead of you, when you know your day will be filled with sorrow and grief? Where do you go from there? How do you find the hope? More importantly, how do you become the beacon of hope for everyone around you?

I write this story as a means of therapy for my soul. It was not until I felt able to write about my family's journey that I could process some of the heart wrenching things we had been through. I write this story for my children, so that they know what happened in the days and months following their father's death. I personally am not able to just shut the book and pretend that it never happened. It was not only that their father's loss of life was immeasurably devastating, but that the way he lived his life was a lesson to us all that needs to be told. Finally, I write this story for all the young widows who might pick up this book. There is hope and light and truth to be found in this crazy world. But it doesn't just come to you; you have to search for it. May you find the truth that you are looking for and the peace that you are meant to have.

Psalm 23 says, "The LORD is my shepherd; I shall not want. He makes me to lie down in green pastures: he leads me beside quiet waters. He restores my soul: he guides me in paths of righteousness for his name's sake. Even *though I walk through the valley of the shadow of death*, I will fear no evil, for you are with me; your rod and your staff they comfort me. You prepare a table before me in the presence of my enemies: you anoint my head with oil; my cup overflows. Surely goodness and love will follow me all the days of my life: and I will dwell in the house of the LORD for ever."

When I read this Psalm, it reminds that God will be the one to restore my broken heart. Even though I am not walking in the shadow of *my* death, as some may read that Psalm to mean, I will always walk in the valley of the shadow of Curt's death—and so will our children. His life and his death will never leave us. It is impossible for a person to touch your soul the way that he touched ours and be able to walk away and forget. Instead, we learn to walk in the valley of the shadow, with our heads held high, looking for the beauty around us and the sun shining down on us from Heaven. This book will hopefully show that we, as a family, have chosen to embrace his life rather than continuously grieve his death. It took many years to get to this point, but we hope to be an inspiration to others who may be experiencing the same pain.

Read this book with an open heart and an open mind. Powerful things happen in your life when you choose to believe. It isn't until you have lost someone so incredibly dear to you that you will have been forced on the quest that I have now been on. Your beliefs are challenged and your faith is shaken. Believing in Heaven is one thing, dear friends; trying to find it to reach your loved one is a *whole* other.

Prologue

"Mom!! Curt is alive!!!"

It was early in the morning, and my sister Kim awoke to her five year old son Ty racing down the stairs to find her. He was frantically trying to relay a message to her, which was his absolute certainty that his Uncle Curt was alive! The look on his face proved that he was beyond sure of himself. Kim instantly felt heartbroken, knowing that what Ty was saying was not (and never could be) true. You see, Ty's uncle had accidentally died three weeks before, at the age of thirty-two, while on a hunting trip. Kim knew that he was not alive, even though Ty was sure he was.

"Oh no, honey, he is not alive", she sadly said to him.

"Yes!! He *IS*! He was just in my room! He just told me that no one needs to stay with Auntie Amy anymore because he is always with her and he is keeping her safe!!" He was so sure of himself that it was hard not to believe him. Kim only wished she could.

"Oh Ty, did you just have a dream about Uncle Curt?" Kim asked.

"NO!! He was in my room! Amy needs to tell everyone that they can go home! He told me, Mom!" Ty exclaimed.

Still trying to find some answers, Kim asked Ty if he *had* seen Curt, what he looked like.

Ty explained that he was standing by his bedroom door, and was wearing his work clothes: his jeans, work boots, and a t-shirt. He said that Curt smiled at him. He was not scared at all because he knew that it was his Uncle Curt. Ty listened to him and then ran down to his mom as soon as he got the message from him, overjoyed that his Uncle Curty was alive!

Kim called me about an hour later, hesitantly explaining to me what had happened. She did not want to upset me, but said that Ty honestly believed that Curt (my husband) had been there with him that morning. Even though Kim promised him over and over that it must have been a dream, he was insisting to her that it was *not* a dream. What he saw was real. Ty said he wanted to go to my house, to prove that Curt was there. Kim was calling me because she wanted me to know ahead of time that this was the situation.

Once Ty was out of Kindergarten that day, Kim drove him to my house. She tried to tell him again that Curt was not alive. He didn't want to hear any of it. As soon as they got there, Ty quickly jumped out of their car and ran into my house. Upon his entering, I also tried to explain to Ty that Curt was not alive, even though it was hard to believe myself. He looked everywhere for him, sure that he had seen him in his room that morning, certain that he was alive. Slowly, as he searched, you could see his face turn from excitement to disbelief. He was so confused and distressed that his Uncle was not there. I could hardly stand to watch him in his defeat.

Later that night, Ty's dad, Jon, tried to explain to Ty that his Uncle Curt was not really alive. Ty stated once again, "Yes he *is*!! Curt will always be alive! He is just invisible to you! But I could see him."

Jon asked, "Can you see him right now?"

Ty replied, "No, Dad, but I could see him in my room this morning!"

I have heard quite often that when a loved one has passed, their spirit will come back to visit the children. Children are pure and unassuming. I believe with all of my heart that Curt was there that morning. He needed to get a message to me. If he had come to me directly, I would have been scared, but Ty was welcoming and excited.

I slept at home by myself for the first time that night. I knew through Ty's message that Curt wanted me to know I could be brave enough because he was there with me always. I called my dad and told him that I would be ok—that everyone could go home, that Curt would keep me safe.

This is where my healing began.

PART ONE

Love

CHAPTER ONE

Meeks Bay, Tahoe

Have you ever met someone in your life, who when they walk into the room, you know they are there? Their presence is significant, their energy is undeniable. This person was my husband, Curtis Alan Conner. He was confident and strong. He wore his whole heart on his sleeve. Because of this, you always knew he was going to say what was on his mind (which was not always a great thing)! None the less, what you saw was what you got. His emotion was raw and genuine. His character was incredibly hard-working and intensely ambitious. His heart was trusting, yet cautious, protective and true. It was an honor to be his partner in this life, even if only for a short time . . . .

*   *   *

FRIDAY, JULY 25, 2008

"What do you mean, they are *not* coming? Oh, I don't think so! They're coming! I'm calling Jon back right now". This was Curt's instant reaction to my sister and brother-in-law's phone call. It was the day we were leaving for our big camping trip at Meeks Bay, Tahoe. Curt and I were already pulling into the campground,

3

our nineteen foot trailer in tow behind us. We were meeting five other couples and their families for a weekend full of adventure. One of those couples was my sister, Kim, and her husband, Jon. They were to be joining us with their two boys, Jake and Ty.

Kim had just called to inform us that while they were packing their camping trailer, Jon noticed a strange smell in the air, similar to sulfur. He did not want to risk driving the hour up to Tahoe and then not be able to fix the problem. What if it was something dangerous that needed to be repaired immediately? He didn't want to chance it.

In Curt's world, if it needed to be fixed, he would fix it. No ifs, ands, or buts about it. He had every tool in the world packed into the tool box in the back of his white Dodge Ram pickup. He knew how to fix just about anything you put in front of him. His solution was that Jon needed to bring the trailer up to Meeks, they would have it fixed within an hour of their arrival, and on the sandy beach drinking a beer within two. What was the problem? I could tell Curt was concerned they weren't going to make it. He grabbed his phone.

"Jonny! Bro, bring your trailer up here. I know exactly what the problem is. It's your water tanks. I have the chemicals to fix it for you as soon as you get it here." Long pause. "Yeh, Jonny! I've got all the tools. Don't worry about it bro! You know I've got it covered. Get up here and let's get camping!"

He hung up and smiled at me. "They're on their way!" All was right in the world again. I'm pretty sure that Jon was expecting that call back from Curt. There is no way Curt was going to tolerate their not camping on a count of a technical issue. And camping without at least one of my sisters and their family was just NOT camping.

One thing that has to be known about my family is that I have three sisters, and the four of us are as close as sisters can get. My twin sister, Carrie, and I are the youngest. Kim is in the middle, and Julie is the oldest. We are either on the phone or with each other once a day. It is such a magnificent coincidence that all of our husbands get along with each other just as well as the sisters do. Julie is married to Pete, Kim to Jon, and Carrie to Brian. The four couples, along with my parents, are together at least once a week—eating dinner, playing games, having a few drinks, and mostly hazing each other and laughing all the while. Our kids total seven in all, and they are like brothers and sisters to each other. Our family is closely knit and proud of it. We are best friends and thankful to have this bond.

So when Kim and Jon said they might not be able to make the camping trip, Curt was really and truly stressed. They were one of the reasons he was so looking forward to this weekend. Jon was one of his best camping buddies and friends. Kim and Curt were truly as close as a brother and sister could be. How could they not come on this well planned out campout?

As each of the families began to arrive, we mapped out our camp spots. There were three single units and one unit that had a double parking spot in it. Side by side, two trailers would have to snuggly fit into these spots with about three feet in between them. Was the campground serious about this? Two cars might park comfortably here, but two camping trailers? Honestly, it was not possible that two camping trailers would actually fit, side by side, in this spot. The campground, we soon discovered, was originally built as a tent campground. So, it actually *was* meant for cars to park here, not trailers. Being a sold out weekend in the campground, we had no choice. We were going to have to park two trailers in that one spot!

5

Most people would look at this situation and panic a bit. That is a loss of some pretty personal space when you can look from your window into the window of the trailer next to you and see their every move. I was praying that Curt did not volunteer us. I also knew my husband well enough to know that if there was a problem, he was going to solve it. So here we go . . . .

"We'll share this spot with Jon and Kim!" Curt proudly announced to our friends! Not only did he volunteer us, but he also excitedly volunteered Jon and Kim!! "It's perfect! Jon won't mind! I am sure Kim won't! We'll back both of our trailers in and set up our camp tables and chairs in one spot! We got it guys! I'll explain it to Jon when he gets here!"

Oh wow, Curt! What a great idea!!! That's wonderful!! And to tell you the truth, this is why Curt and I got along so well. I actually found it humorous. While Curt was genuinely excited about his plan, I was extremely amused at the idea of him telling Jon that we were going to share this one spot. I couldn't wait for Kim and Jon to get there. While I helped Curt back our trailer into one of the two spots, I kept a close lookout for Kim and Jon's truck so I could have front row to this little "show". When I caught a glimpse of the silver Toyota Tundra, my heart jumped with happiness! Let the games begin!

"They're here!!" I shouted to Curt. He was busy leveling off our trailer when they arrived. He instantly left his task to meet Jon at his truck. Of course, I followed along to catch his reaction.

"OK, Jonny. Slight change of plans! There is one spot that is going to need to share two trailers side by side. So I told everyone we would take that spot". I could see Jon's face turn from excitement to a touch of worry. He glanced around the campground, passing over our trailer that was already parked. Surely this was not where he was talking about.

"Where's the spot? Will we be pretty close to each other?" Jon asked.

When Curt pointed out our camping trailer, and Jon got a look at the tiny space where his trailer would also be sitting, he calmly replied, "Oh, no we are not! Curt! There is no way! We won't even be able to open our camper door! Those spots were not meant for trailers! No way man! Impossible!"

I looked at Kim and burst into laughter. Our spot was one of those things that you had to see to believe. Looking at Kim's face I could tell she was feeling a combination of things: relieved to finally be up there, entertained by Curt's confidence and constant planning abilities, and stressed by the look on Jon's face. I, of course, was still giddily taking it all in. These moments are the kind of thing that we would look back and laugh at.

As a side note, Kim, Jon, and I all knew that Curt was going to make it happen. He had that look in his eye and the determination on his face. We either needed to jump on and enjoy the ride or sit back and watch the show, because he was going to move forward regardless.

After much coaxing, Curt talked Jon into parking his trailer next to ours. Let me tell you, it took a village to get it parked. All of the guys from our group came over to help. If you have ever had the pleasure of backing a camping trailer into a camping spot, you would know that it is not as easy as it looks. It takes a lot of skill and practice to do this smoothly. Add in the fact that there is only so much room on all sides or you're going to crash it, and it makes the situation a little bit more stressful.

Jon was really feeling the pressure and knew that it was only going to happen inch by inch. He would pull forward, crank his steering wheel to the right, back in an inch—then park it and get out and look. Then he would get in, crank the wheel back to the left, and pull forward an inch. ANY person I know, including myself, who has tried to park a trailer, knows how nerve wracking it can be to get it right. Jon's circumstances were multiplied by ten. I could see Curt, however, was getting impatient. He had a look in his eyes that he knew he could get that trailer in within no time.

Curt approached Jon's window and said, "Jonny—I got it! I'll get it back in there. You guide me back in." Jon knew there was a slight problem with this. Anyone who knew Curt, knew there was no doubt that he was capable; however when Curt drove somebody else's car, his motto was, "Drive it like you stole it," followed by one of his deep infectious laughs. *Not* comforting when that car is yours. Jon eased cautiously out of his seat, and Curt hopped right in!

Kim, sitting in the passenger seat, warned him to be careful for the tree on the left. He laughed and said, "It ain't my truck!"

She stated, matter of fact, "Yes, but it is *mine!*"

He looked at her with a straight face and said, "Oh, yeah, sorry!"

By the time the door was shut, he had already thrown the truck in reverse and glided right back into that sandwich of a spot before we even knew what he was thinking. He did hit a few tree branches on the side of the trailer here and there. But before you could say, "Curt slow down!!" the job was done! No guessing, inching, stressing, or planning for Curt. It was *always* either, "Go Big or Go Home".

And there you had it! Two camping trailers parked within inches of each other, a stressed out brother-in-law, a triumphant husband, an unsure sister, a group of excited kids, and a weekend full of adventure waiting to be had.

CHAPTER TWO

A Surprising Visitor

Meeks Bay, Lake Tahoe could not have been a more stunning setting for this unforgettable vacation. The campground is located off of Highway 89 on the west shore of the famously beautiful Lake Tahoe. At 6, 225 feet in elevation, it is home to 40 tent and RV spots. The sandy white beach, with its crystal clear blue waters, was within walking distance of our campsites. Meeks Bay sits in between two beautiful California state parks with plenty of opportunities for hiking and backpacking. Our group, however, had one plan for our weekend: camping and relaxing on the beach with our families, which is exactly what we did as soon as we got our camp set up.

Setting up camp was no small feat for the Conner family. It actually became ritualistic, in a sense. Once the trailer was unhitched from Curt's truck, he leveled it, placed down the jacks for stability and then the chalk under the tires for security. He would then hook up the battery to the ridiculously expensive generator (sorry Curt, it was) to make sure we had a charge, fill the tanks with water, put up the canopy, set up the outdoor stereo speakers, and put down the steps. Then to unloading the back of the truck . . .

People used to say that when we pulled up to camping, everyone knew it was us just by looking at the back of Curt's truck. This was ALL Curt's doing, not mine. He would proudly admit this, too. It was packed to the brim with kids' bikes, adult bikes, a bike trailer, several coolers (with CONNER written in permanent marker on the inside), camp chairs, beach chairs, rafts, and horseshoes. All of this was tied down with Bunjee cords and ropes, just in case something were to fly out unexpectedly while we were driving. Oh my, it was a real Sanford and Son sight! He loved it, though! He was a man of many toys. He felt the more toys, the more fun that was meant to be had. Packing the back of that truck was a very involved process and he loved every minute of it.

While he worked on unpacking all of this, I was in charge of the inside of the trailer. I always unpacked all of the kids' clothes, put away all of the food for the trip, and made sure the inside of the trailer was organized and clean. Curt was in charge of the outside of the trailer and all of the manly stuff. I took on the inside of the trailer and all of the womanly and mother hen type of stuff. In addition, while Curt was tending to the outside of the trailer, it was also my job to watch over and entertain our kids to make sure they were safe and happy and excited to be camping.

Our kids, Mckenna and Luke, were ages four and two, respectively, on this particular weekend. They were thrilled to be camping with their little friends and two of their cousins. They were especially thrilled now that their cousins' trailer was within hands reach of ours.

Camping was such a joy to all of the kids in our family. This was a time when they were allowed to get dirty, which they did from head to toe. They were able to eat almost whatever they wanted, within reason. Their endless days consisted of running around and playing until dark. Follow this with s'mores and marshmallows by the fire and life could not be any better.

Once the trailer was unpacked and the kids were ready to go, we headed down to join our friends by the water. Shade tents were in place, beach chairs were set, coolers were stocked, music was playing, kids were splashing and the adults were relaxing. I remember looking around and thinking that this is what life is all about. These moments. I know for our family, camping is a way for us all to take time out from the real world. You can not bottle up the excitement that comes with camping in our circle of friends and family.

We spent the rest of the day at the beach, and then headed back up to camp to get ready for dinner. After the kids were washed up, fed, and had devoured their s'mores, it was off to bed for them. Another bonus to camping is that once kids agree to go to bed (after begging not to) they will usually fall right to sleep. They are so wiped out that they stumble under their covers, close their eyes, and they are asleep within minutes.

At this point in the evening, I usually was the one who would stay in the trailer with the kids to make sure they would fall asleep and didn't need anything. Curt always wished that I would put them down and then come out and join him at the campfire. However, I would usually lie down, open a good book or magazine with the intent of actually reading it, and then fall asleep. I am just being honest. If I were living life on the Mommy edge, I would've put the kids down and joined the rest of the adults for a few hours of campfire stories and a view of the millions of stars in the night sky. If I had only known then what I know now, I would have done just that. Hindsight really is 20/20.

As I sat in the trailer, thankful that our kids were now asleep, I heard a noise outside the door. Was that the cooler? I was pretty sure that it was! It was the creaking of the cooler opening right outside our trailer door. I have to say that I was quite a bit perturbed because I knew how much beer the men of our group had in their cooler up by the fire. Could they have possibly finished all of it and were now tapping into the supply in our cooler? That was a bit much, didn't they think? I knew we were camping, and this was a part of the campfire fun, but really? Was it necessary to need to get more?

After a few minutes, I could hear men's voices outside of our trailer. They were talking pretty loudly next to the window. This was kind of ridiculous! They were going to wake the kids up. What was Curt thinking? Didn't he know how golden it was for the kids to be sleeping soundly? I couldn't take it anymore. I quietly swung the trailer door open to ask (as nicely as possible) for them to keep it down!

To my astonishment, Curt and two of our friends were standing at the door with disbelief on their faces. One of our friends, Mike, had a Coleman headlamp on, which is like wearing a small, round flashlight stuck to your forehead. Our other friend, Mark, had a flashlight in hand.

Curt, also wearing a Coleman headlamp on his head (which always cracked me up), looked at me with eyes as big as I had ever seen them. He excitedly exclaimed, "Amy, Bear!!! Did you see it? There was a bear in our cooler! It took my pepper jack cheese!"

I knew by the look on his face that he was not kidding. The sound of the lid to the cooler opening was not Curt and his friends after all. It was a bear! A big black bear was digging for food in our cooler within feet of me and I thought it was Curt! It effortlessly wandered right up to our cooler, creaked open its door, found what he was looking for, and wandered off into the dark forest.

It is common for black bears to roam the campgrounds at night in search of food. All coolers are supposed to be kept in locked storage containers that the campgrounds provide. The guys could hear the bear in ours, obviously not locked up, and came to check it out.

This is exactly the type of excitement that Curt was looking for! After the guys relived their moment with me, made sure the cooler was locked up, and double checked that our trailer was securely closed, they headed eagerly back up to the camp fire. I had to laugh. They were like a bunch of Boy Scouts looking for their next adventure. As I settled in again with my book, I could only imagine what else our weekend had in store for us.

*   *   *

SATURDAY, JULY 26, 2008

The next morning was filled with chatter about the bear. The kids wished they had been able to catch a glimpse of it. The guys were proud to have gotten so close to it. I was still a bit uneasy that this bear was so close to me and I had no idea. It couldn't have hurt me inside of the trailer. It is not as if I was in a tent, but the thought of it being right next to me made me wonder how close the bears actually get to us while we are sitting at night by the campfires. I was surprised we hadn't remembered to put the cooler in the locking bins before it turned dark. You'd better believe we were going to that night. We didn't need another close encounter with one of Tahoe's hungry bears.

After Curt and Jon made the customary breakfast burritos with eggs, chorizo, and salsa (minus the pepper jack cheese), we joined our friends in getting ready to head down to the beach.

13

Our plan was to spend the entire day there. We had several shade tents up for cover from the sun and plenty of sunscreen for the kids. I knew we were going to need the cooler to be fully stocked. I still needed to pack extra clothes for the kids, sandwiches and drinks for lunch, and sand toys for the beach. Already feeling a bit overwhelmed, I could see our son Luke warily approaching the trailer. I knew just by looking at him what he needed.

"Mommy?" he asked in a drawn out tone.

"Yes, Lukey", I stated in my most patient voice.

"I need to go potty!" he stated painfully. I already knew this was not going to be an easy task. Luke had an extremely difficult time trying to go the bathroom. Potty training for him was not as easy as it was for his sister. It was an exasperating experience for me, too. In the back of my mind, I knew our friends were getting ready to walk down to the beach and I still needed to finish packing up. Combine this with a little boy who needed me to sit with him and a husband who was anxious to make this all happen within minutes, and it equaled a wife who was about to blow her top.

Poor Curt! He didn't even know what was about to hit him. He stepped up into the trailer and said, "Come on Amy! Are you ready? Everyone is about to leave! Aren't you ready to go yet!?"

Oh, and the fury was unleashed! "Are you kidding with me right now? While you are out there talking to all your buddies about your big scary bear, I am in here trying to clean up from breakfast, make the lunches, get the beach bag together, dress the kids, and pack it all up! Now I have Luke in here trying to go to the bathroom. Do you know how much time goes into trying to help him go to the bathroom? No, of course you don't, because you never sit with him and talk him through this whole potty training thing! I do! So don't come in here and ask me if I am ready! It would be nice if you just helped me out a little bit, *Curt!"*

Curt, looking like he had been hit by a train, slowly backed out of the trailer. He literally did not even say a thing back to me. It even surprised me that I reacted this way. He was such a great helper when it came to packing things up and getting the kids ready. We definitely were a great team. One hardly ever carried more weight than the other. He knew I was having a moment and I just needed some time to cool off. As he was walking, dazed and confused, away from the trailer, he ran into Kim.

"Hey, Kim, will you do me a favor? Will you go into my trailer and see if Amy is mad at me? She just got mad, but I am not sure if she is actually mad at *me*. Just please go in there and check the situation out. OK?"

Kim laughed, "OK, Curt. I'll go check it out. I'll be right back." Of course Kim came into the trailer and checked the situation out for Curt. She knew I was not mad at him, just as much as he did. I was just overwhelmed. I was having a Mommy moment. We feel sometimes, as mothers, that we do everything for everyone all of the time. There is hardly a moment that is given just to us. That is how I was feeling. Inundated with life's everyday tasks, swamped with everybody else's needs. I needed a break and Curt just so happened to pass through that moment of frustration at the wrong time.

Kim reassured Curt that everything was fine. They gathered the kids and the coolers and headed down to the beach without me. This gave me a chance to gather myself. Obviously I had lost my cool and Curt knew it. Of course, I knew I was justified in my feelings, but Curt did not need to be the recipient of my backlash. I knew what I really wanted was to have fun on this trip and create new, meaningful memories. So I decided to take a deep breath,

15

freshen up, put on the cutest bikini I had, along with a smile on my face, and head down to spend some much needed time with my family and friends.

As I was walking down to the shore, I could see Curt suspiciously watching me out of the corner of his eye. Was I going to be upset with him? Was I going to give him the cold shoulder? Was I going to say anything to him at all? In our eight years together, we had been in plenty of arguments that could have ended in any one of those scenarios. Instead, I did just the opposite. I walked right by him, smiled, told him that I loved him, gave him a hug and a kiss, and headed down towards my friends. I didn't even turn around to see the shocked look on his face.

This is such a difficult thing for us, as women, to do sometimes: Let go of an argument, admit that we were wrong, show any sign of weakness. I know it always was for me with Curt. There are times in our life when it is necessary to just let it go—when it compromises your ability to be in love and be loved, when it compromises the enjoyment of your time spent together, when you don't even know it is your last few days you will ever get to spend with the ones you love. Something inside of me told me that this was one of those times to just to let it go.

CHAPTER THREE

Testing the Waters

While the ladies relaxed with the kids by the lake, the gentlemen played a game called "Cornhole". It is very similar to horseshoes, except the players use bean bags instead. The bean bags are tossed about 30 feet across to a platform with a small round opening where they are meant to fall. Three points are earned if the bag falls in the hole, and one point if it lands on the platform. Curt loved this game, mostly because he loved to haze his opponents and tell them how much better of a player he was than them. He was constantly chatting in their ears, and they back at him. The first team to earn twenty-one points wins the game. It is a lot of fun to play and can be very entertaining to watch.

At one point in the game, I remember that Luke wandered up in the sand to where Curt was playing. As soon as Curt saw him, he bent down to Luke's eye level and put his arm around his waist. This is the way Curt responded to our kids at all times. He spoke to them eye to eye, never once raising his voice at them. He used to joke around before we had children and say, "My kids will never misbehave. If they do, I am going to give them a good spanking!" He never once spanked either Mckenna or Luke. I was definitely more of the authoritarian of the two of us. He would even say, "Oh, Amy, please don't put my little goose in time out."

His "little goose" was Mckenna. He also called her "Roses" because her middle name is Rose. Mckenna could just look at her Daddy and his heart would melt around her little finger. Anyone who has ever been able to witness the love between a father and his daughter knows what I am talking about. It is an unbreakable bond if a Daddy respects, loves, and provides for his little girl the way that Curt did for Mckenna. When she was an infant, she would sit in our window by the front door and just wait for him to get home. He would walk into the door and she would jump up and down and squeal in delight. He would pick her up into his arms and she would instantly put her head on his shoulder and put her thumb in her mouth. It was like he was her blankie, her comfort.

As Mckenna got older, Curt would go every few weeks to the florist and buy her flowers. He would come home, with her excitedly waiting, walk in the door and announce, "I'm home!" Mckenna would run out to him and he would drop to his knees on the carpet. He'd say, "Mckenna, what does Daddy have for you behind his back?"

She would yell, "Flowers, Daddy! Can I have them please?" And out would come the most beautiful flowers. Of course we would need to go and find a vase for her, and upstairs they would go to her room. Oh how that man loved his little girl—and then came his little boy.

Curt was as proud of Luke as he was of Mckenna. I believe in my heart that Curt looked at Luke and saw himself as a little boy. He wanted to give him everything that he never had. When looking into Luke's little eyes, he found such joy in knowing he was going to provide him with stability and love, family and tradition. For the first time in his life, he was truly touched by the bond of a father and a son. This time, being the father and not the forgotten son, he found it astonishing that there were parents out there who could ever abandon their children the way that he was as a child. His love for his children was his main priority in his life, and he strived to show it to them every day.

Luke was only able to witness that love for two years, but in that short time, Curt created a lifetime of memories. He bought him his first bike, took him on his first motorcycle, and flew his first kite with him—just to name a few. A few months before he passed away, Curt took Luke fishing during one of our camping trips. Luke had never held a fishing pole before, and at the age of two he definitely needed help. Curt sat with him, just the two of them, and held that pole with him, hand over hand. Luke was so proud to be there with his Daddy's arm wrapped around him showing him all of his love and attention.

Curt teaching Luke how to fish for the first time.

And now here we were again, in Tahoe, with Curt's arm wrapped around Luke's waist while he played his game. I felt positively and overwhelmingly complete as a family. I watched as my husband and son were enjoying their time together. My daughter and I were playing in the sand while listening to some music. The day was beautiful and I knew the evening would be, too. Everything in our lives seemed to be falling into such a great place. Life did not always come so easy to Curt and me. We had to work extremely hard to find this comfort in our lives, so I felt thankful and blessed to witness this moment.

As I found myself lost in this thought, I glanced over to the shore and realized that both of the paddleboards our group had with us were not in use. Our friends, Mike and Becky, had brought two paddleboards (which looked like giant surfboards) to the lake with us for everyone to try. Mike, owning the paddleboard company, taught everyone how to stand on the board and balance while paddling with an oar. It was much harder than it looked. Time after time, people in our group tried to stand on the board and balance, only to fall off into the water. Even the kids rode on them, fell off of them, and climbed right back up to try again.

I had not yet attempted to stand up on the board because I didn't want everyone to watch me fall off. Call me crazy, it is just how I am. When I slowly glanced around to my left, and then to my right, I realized that no one was paying attention. Now was my chance.

I quietly said to Kim, "I am going to take the paddleboard out on the water and try to stand up on it. Will you please make sure that Luke and Mckenna are ok? I don't want them to realize I am gone". Truth be told, not only was Luke clingy with me and wouldn't want me out on the water without him, but I also did not want anyone to watch me try out this new task. I wanted to go out on my own and see if I could do it without any pressure from the sidelines.

As I grabbed a board and headed out, I was thankful for some time to myself. The day was so beautiful and the lake was crystal clear. Sitting on the board, I paddled out close to the buoy. I looked onto the shore and saw Luke still standing with Curt, while Mckenna played in the sand next to Kim. The guys were still playing their game and the girls were all preoccupied. Perfect! Now was the time.

I had to talk myself into standing up and trying to balance on the board. My thoughts went a little something like this: "OK Amy, you can do this! All you have to do is place your feet evenly on the board and stand up. If you fall off (into this ice cold water) you just climb back on and try again. You'll regret it if you don't! Now come on! Stand up!!"

I slowly climbed up onto my knees. Even in doing this, I could feel the board wobble underneath me. I remember Mike telling me that the board was wide and hard to tip over. I also remember all of my friends who had already fallen off trying to balance while standing up. So here I stayed for a few minutes, up on my knees, trying to talk myself into standing up. In my mind, no one was watching me and I could take as much time as I needed. Little did I know, however, that at this exact same moment, Kim had headed up to where Curt was playing his game and pointed me out on the water. She wanted him to see that I was trying to stand up on the board, knowing he would be proud of me. So I had a bit more of an audience than I realized.

Feeling confident, I pulled one foot up onto the board causing it tip down on one side and then the other. I kept my other knee firmly on the board which allowed me to steady it. My hands were wrapped around the handle of the paddle, which was laid across the board in front of me. Now the hard part . . . putting my weight into my hands on the paddle, I pulled my other foot up onto the board and was now in a low squat. The board started to shake underneath me while I positioned my feet on the outside edges of it. If I was going to fall, this would be the time. I knew if I could not find my center on this board, I was going into the water for sure!

With shaky legs, I slowly stood up. The paddle still in both hands, I felt sure of myself and ready to try to move. Shifting the paddle into my right hand, I lowered the end of it into the water. Once I felt the weight of the paddle on the right side of the board, my center was thrown off. I tried to counter balance by leaning to the other side, but this only made matters worse. Panicking, I sat back down on the board as quickly as I could. In what took me about five minutes to stand up, only took me about fifteen seconds to sit back down.

Wanting to get up and try again, I looked up to make sure no one was watching me. What I saw took me a bit by surprise. On the other paddle board, gliding slowly towards me, was Curt! Sitting on his board, he moved his paddle from one side of the board to the other, coasting steadily in my direction. He had a great big smile on his face. As he got closer, he shouted to me, "That was perfect Amy!! Now all you need to do is learn how to paddle the board forward!!"

That was easy for him to say! Curt took to paddle boarding like a duck takes to water. The first time he got on the board, he jumped right up on it, and paddled away like he had been riding for years. His first time out, he was gone for about an hour, just cruising around the shoreline of Tahoe. He loved it and thought it was so much fun! He is part of the reason why so many others fell off each time they tried. He had made it look so easy, that they underestimated the difficulty in finding a balance on the board. So when he said that all I needed to do was just learn how to paddle, I laughed!

"Curt, I am not going to try to paddle while you watch me! I just wanted to come out here and try this without *anyone* watching me! You make it look so easy, but that was hard to stand up! I thought the board was going to tip underneath me!"

"I know, but I was so excited you were out here trying. I thought I would come and help! I'm sorry! I'll go back into shore if you want some more time to yourself". I honestly found it so charming that he wanted to help me, that I couldn't resist having him out there in the water with me.

"No, I don't want you to go back in. I'll try to do this again later, but I would like to stay out here for a little while longer." We sat on our boards, floating next to each other in the water. Curt kept his hand on my board so we didn't drift away from each other.

"Isn't it beautiful out here?" Curt asked. "I honestly don't know why we would camp anywhere else. This is the perfect place for our family to be. The campground is fun, it is right next to the water, and Tahoe is so beautiful! I love it here!"

"It is so nice, and so much fun! Everyone is having such a great time! The kids love sitting here by the water. It is perfect," I added. For about five more minutes we had a quiet conversation floating out on the water. We talked a little more about the campground, our campsite, and what our plans were for dinner. Having two kids, it's rare to find opportunities to sit quietly and just talk. The ability to sit out on the boards and connect was so special to us. Even in the moment, I felt very thankful for that little gift.

Paddling back into shore, I suddenly felt like I was confident enough to try to stand on the paddle board again. In my mind, I was saying to myself, "Are you crazy? Everyone on the shore would be watching you! You don't want to fall in front of all of these people do you? Wait until you have a moment to yourself again!" But my heart was saying, "You can do it! Just stand up one more time and try to paddle! If it's too hard, just sit back down!" I looked at Curt and said, "I'm going to try once more. Please don't make a big deal out of it. I am going to sit back down if I can't do it. OK?"

Curt's face lit up. "OK, Amy! Remember put your feet wide on the board and once you start to paddle, it will make you balance easier!" I slowly stood up on the board once more, Curt watching quietly, shifting the paddle to my right hand again. Putting my left hand above my right hand, I began to push the paddle board into a forward movement and glide through the water. I'd like to say it looked graceful and practiced, but it felt awkward and unstable. I was able to keep my momentum for about twenty seconds until I realized my right leg had tipped the board. Feeling off center again, I quickly sat down.

"You did it, Amy!! You were paddling through the water!! Great job, Amy!! You did it!" Curt was so excited for me! It was as if I had won a gold medal at the Olympics. You could see it in his face, he was so proud of me!

Still feeling defeated, though, I said, "I know I did paddle, Curt! But I only stood up for a minute and then lost it! I didn't really paddle board. All that I did was just stand up!"

Curt looked at me, right into my eyes, and stated ecstatically, "Amy, that doesn't *matter*! You did such a great job!! You weren't even going to try, and you stood up and paddled through the water! You did it!! I'm so excited! That's all you had to do! You did it!"

*He was right. I *did*! Thank you, Curt!!

24

CHAPTER FOUR

Best of Intentions

The rest of our afternoon was filled with laughter and fun. My twin sister, Carrie, drove up for the day to join us. She brought her 4 week old baby girl, Ashtyn, and her son Tanner. My sister Julie's son, Dylan, joined them. We all sat down by the water's edge with our friends and their kids and enjoyed the day. Several times, Curt and I would sit on the paddleboards and load them up with all of the kids. We'd ride them around the lake, which they loved. At one point Curt and our friend Mark had a "pirate water fight" with all of the boys, splashing each other with the paddles. Kim and I took turns sitting under the canopy to hold our brand new baby niece, Ashtyn. It was the perfect ending to a perfect day.

After gathering up our beach items and making our way back to camp, we all pitched in to prepare and serve dinner. Once it was cleaned up, the adults set up all of our chairs around the campfire where our eager children were ready for some s'mores. The night was quickly falling upon us, and we were ready for an evening of fun. With plenty of marshmallows, chocolate, and graham crackers to go around, the kids and adults filled up on one tasty treat after another. Once the kids could eat no more, the parents began to take their little ones to bed.

Amy and Curt on the paddleboards loaded up with kids at Meeks Bay.

At this time, I normally stood up and started the process in getting the kids to bed. Parents, you know what I am talking about—when you announce to your children that it is time to wrap up their evening. It's the begging, the bartering, and the pleading that we endure each time our kids are asked to go to bed. It's not until their heads actually hit the pillow that they are out like a light.

On most occasions, I would say (in the sweetest voice), "OK, Mckenna and Luke—we need to go get our pajamas on." This generally would be matched with some whining and persuasive reasoning to "please, please, please stay up a little longer". In which my tone would become a bit firmer and I would remind them that they had already had a fun, full day and now it was dark outside and time for bed.

Instead, on this star-filled evening, I just stayed in my chair with Mckenna on my lap, and relaxed by the fire. Curt sat with Luke on his lap in the chair to the right of us. The kids both had cozy blankets wrapped around them and smiles on their little tucked-in faces. They never really got to stay up late at the campfire, especially not to where they stayed awake longer than some of the adults. Even their Uncle Jon finally said, "Goodnight everyone! I'm heading to bed! If anyone sees a bear tonight, make sure to wake me up so I get to see it this time!"

To which Curt retorted, "Ya, Bro—don't worry, I'm tossin' a raw steak on your trailer step. The bear's coming for *you* tonight!" followed by a deep, mischievous laugh. Everyone around the fire laughed, but none of us would have put it past him.

Curt leaned over to me and asked if I needed help taking the kids to bed. To his surprise, I said, "No, let's just let them sit out here with us for a while. They can fall asleep wrapped up in the blankets right here". Curt was so pleased that I said this to him. Being that the kids were always on a routine, he never wanted to stray from that. But to Curt, camping should have always been the exception to this rule. After about fifteen minutes, both of them were asleep in our arms. It was so cozy. Curt and I were able to hang out together by the fire with all of our friends and the kids got to sit by the warmth of the flames under a zillion stars in the night sky.

As the evening wore on, more of our friends started heading to bed. One of the husbands in our group, Steve, had decided he was going to head back to his camp. The sky was pitch black and he needed a flashlight to find his way. Before he could even make it into the dark brush, he stumbled upon a large surprise! He was back to the campfire before we even knew he was gone with a look on his face that explained it all. "There's a BIG bear, right *there* by Curt and Amy's trailer!!!" He was pointing in the direction of our campsite!

Within five seconds, Curt (with Luke in his arms), a few of our friends, and I (with Mckenna in my arms) were up and headed towards our trailer. Right as we got to there, Steve shone the flashlight on the paved road, and there it was! A giant black bear was walking on the path past Kim and Jon's trailer and then turned to walk up towards some more campsites. He slowly waddled up the mountain, wandering aimlessly next to tents and trailers. At one point, he stopped and turned around, staring right into the flashlight's glare as if to say, "Yeah, I see you! Big deal!", and then gradually turned back around and kept walking.

I was so excited about the bear that I had forgotten to get Kim and Jon. Curt looked back at me and said, "Amy, go get Jon up so he can see it!" I quickly ran over, squeezed in between our two trailers, banged on their window and told them to hurry if they wanted to see it. Kim flew out of her trailer, hoping to catch a glimpse of it, but she missed it. She was so disappointed that she wasn't in time. Jon slept through the whole thing. Curt was beyond ecstatic, and I was curious how a bear ended up in the Conner camp two nights in a row . . . .

*   *   *

SUNDAY, JULY 27TH, 2008

For the second morning now, the camp was abuzz about the bear! It was "amazing that a bear would come to camp two nights in a row!!" Some were assuming that it must be common for the bears to come down often into the camps at night! Or was it? Why else would we have already seen two? After much prodding, I discovered the reason why—and it was not a coincidence.

Curt finally confessed . . . he was so excited to see the bear the first night that he tried to lure the bear in the second night. On the hitch of our trailer, he placed a bunch of grapes to see if another bear would visit. He figured he would know in the morning whether or not a bear had been there if the grapes were gone. He didn't actually think that we would see the bear. The campsites warn against this and do not want bears wandering in the sites at night in search of food. Curt was very well aware of this and was not trying to "break the law" set by the campground. He was just so excited to see the bear the night before that he wanted to see if it would come back.

I just have to say this—my husband did not stop and ponder and think about most things he did in life, he just did it. If he wanted something, and it was within reason, he got it. If he wanted to go somewhere, he went. If he wanted to try something new, he tried. If he wanted to buy something, he bought it. He'd think of the repercussions later. There wasn't time for that in the here and now. Life was meant for living to the fullest at all times. So when he placed those grapes for the bear to eat, he honestly thought that it was a great, fun idea—something he wanted to try, and he did! I always had to shake my head and laugh (sometimes) at his ambition. No wonder he wanted to escort the kids and me to the trailer at bedtime the night before! He didn't want us to cross paths with his little "experiment". It was all beginning to make sense!

Being our last day at camp, most of our friends began to pack up and get ready to leave. Knowing that they had to get ready for a new work week, they wanted to get home with plenty of time to unpack and prepare. I still had five days left until I started my first day at my new job. I had just transferred that summer to teach at a new school in a new program. After nine years teaching first and second grade, I was ready for a new challenge. I was going to be teaching a Pre-Kindergarten class for children with special needs. I had been working on my new classroom all summer long and knew I was not going back to work again before I started my official first day on that Friday. So I was excited to stay and relax.

Curt and I had discussed that he was going to make it a light week at work, as well. He was leaving in three days to go on his annual hunting trip. So we had plenty of time to pack up our campsite to go home. Kim and Jon and a few of our friends decided to go down to the water one last time before heading home. We did not want to rush the ending to such a peaceful weekend.

So that is just what we did! There were a lot of great memories made that afternoon, including the kids climbing on the rocks near the water and searching for crawdads. I have a great picture of Curt with his arm around Mckenna. He is holding up one of the crawdads that the kids had in their buckets. They both are smiling and enjoying their time together. I am thankful to have this picture to remind us all of that day.

Curt and Mckenna with the crawdad they caught at Meeks Bay.

At about 3:00, we decided it was time to go back to our campsite and get ready to go. My parents were celebrating their

40th wedding anniversary on that day and our entire family was meeting at Jon and Kim's house to celebrate with a champagne toast and some horderves. We realized we weren't even going to have enough time to go home first. We were going to need to head straight to this event from camping.

I was busily gathering all of our supplies and camping gear when Curt approached me and stopped me in the process. We were standing in a beautiful section of our campsite, beneath several pine trees, surrounded by a clear blue sky. He put his arms around my waist and said, "Amy, I just need you to know something. I am so proud of you this weekend. You have made me feel so happy. You stayed each day, all day, at the lake with everyone. You got out there yesterday and tried to paddleboard. You looked so cute in your bathing suit and so brave while you were trying. You let the kids stay up late at the campfire, which made it possible for you to stay out later, too—and for the kids to be able to see the bear. You helped us catch crawdads and didn't mind that we stayed all day at the lake today. I have loved every minute of this weekend with you. I love you."

My heart melted. There was not a day in my life with Curt that went by that he did not compliment me or tell me how much he loved me. I always wished I could better show him how much I loved him the way he so easily did for me. This conversation was different, though. It was a moment that I will never forget. He was genuinely needing me to know that he admired my effort to create unforgettable memories with our family. I thanked him and told him that I loved him, too. We stood and held each other for what seemed like an eternity. I felt so at peace with where we were in our lives and so did he. I remember taking a deep breath, with my head on his chest, and just wanting to melt into him. It was a storybook ending to an already perfect weekend.

CHAPTER FIVE

Our Last Family Memory

We pulled into town about five minutes before the start of my parents' anniversary celebration and walked into Jon and Kim's house, the last to arrive. It was funny that Curt and I both still had on our camping clothes and the kids were a mess. Everyone else in the family was dressed appropriately for the celebration. The only thing that really ever matters in our family is that we are all together, so I knew it wouldn't be a problem.

I watched Curt open the slider into the backyard and for a moment it passed through my mind that he looked *so* handsome. He had his black Titleist visor on (sunglasses sitting on top), his new white paddleboard shirt that Mike gave him, his dark blue boarding swim shorts and his flip flop sandals. He looked happy, relaxed, and handsome. As he stepped into the backyard to play basketball with our nephews, a sense of happiness overwhelmed me.

I was also feeling so proud of my parents to be celebrating such an incredible milestone in their lives together. It is such a rarity these days that people are able to last in the union of marriage for twenty years or more, let alone forty. It was so important for them to share this moment with all of their daughters, son-in-laws, and grandchildren. In all, we equaled seventeen. There could not have been more love in that room on that night.

After a while of chatting, we gathered everyone in the kitchen and had a champagne (apple juice for the kids) toast to my parents. Pete gave the toast, in which he spoke of how proud all of their daughters were of their anniversary. Curt, needing to jump in at this point, said, "Hey don't forget about the brothers!" He always loved to get a word in edgewise. We all had a laugh and finished toasting my parents' legacy. As it neared the kids' bedtimes, we began to gather our kids to go home. I remember a feeling of such contentment that night. It was the last time we would all be together again as a family unit. I would not see all of my sisters, their families, and my parents again until when we learned of Curt's death, just four days later.

*   *   *

Once Curt and I got Mckenna and Luke into bed, we sat down on the couch in our downstairs family room to relax and watch television. The program that appeared on our TV was a news story regarding the passing of Randy Pausch. Randy was a professor at Carnegie Mellon where he delivered his "last lecture" in front of a packed auditorium. It had become a tradition for chosen professors to give a lecture upon retiring that summed up all of the most important lessons they could share. Randy, however, gave his lecture in September of 2007, just a month after he was told he only had three to six months to live. He battled with pancreatic cancer. The Last Lecture, called "Really Achieving your Childhood Dreams" became a media sensation, in which was then turned into a best selling book.

We watched in sadness as this story unfolded in front of us. He died just a few days before our viewing this show, on July 25, 2008, at the implausibly young age of 47. He left behind his wife and their three young children. He lived his life in a way that he could leave them with a legacy of his love and lessons of his morals. It was just so heart breaking that his family was left to live this life without him.

After the show was over, Curt turned off the TV and said to me, "I am so sad for him *and* his family! I can't believe that he knew he was leaving them. What would that feel like to know he was going to have to leave them? And now those three little children have to live without their father?? What will his wife do? What will the kids do—without him?" He was truly moved by what he had seen. When you have a wife and children, as did Curt, that you love and provide for, the realization of this family's fate becomes so much more real.

We all just need to hold on tight to the ones that we love, and that is exactly what Curt did. That night in bed, Curt cuddled up to me, and wrapped his arms around me—just a little tighter than usual. I could tell that he was so sad for this man, Randy, and the fact that he would never be able to hug his wife this tight again. It makes me cry to think that Curt would suffer the same fate. Unlike Randy, Curt's loss was without warning. Either way, it is unbearable to conceive. Curt was sad for Randy's family's loss, which ironically would also be his family's loss—just days away.

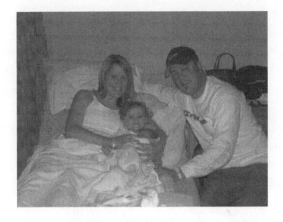

Our family on the day Luke was born. Happy memories.

MONDAY, JULY 28-TUESDAY JULY 29, 2008

The next two days flew by for me. I stayed home with the kids while Curt prepared his business for the time he would be spending away hunting. Curt and I owned a construction company by the name of "American Concrete, Inc." where he and his employees laid patios, foundations, sidewalks, and driveways. He and I built this company from the ground up, about five years prior, out of our home. It took a lot of work and determination to build a small business into a successful entity.

I remember Curt approaching me about starting this business. It was the year our daughter Mckenna was born. We were renting a small house and he was working for a local concrete company. He had been working as a laborer, pouring concrete, since he was eighteen years old. It was all he knew. At twenty-seven years of age, he was ready to be his own boss. He didn't want to work for anyone else. He wanted to open his own business and become

35

successful doing what he knew best. It was going to be a lot of work, he warned me. It was going to take a lot of time to get it up and running, but this is what he wanted to do.

"Will you please help me and support me in this?" he asked.

I had no doubt in my mind that Curt would make the business work. He was not the kind of guy to just sit around and hope that things would happen for him. Before he had even talked to me, he had an application for a business license, a contractor's license, and a business bank account. He worked day and night on getting the business up and running. The only thing he needed the most help with was the finances. He wanted me to run his payroll, liabilities, taxes, and contracts through Quickbooks. I started learning the program as soon as I could. By trial and error, we got it all worked out. Before I knew it, American Concrete was born.

We created a logo and researched our means of advertisement. Our equipment was purchased, and finally our employees were hired. I was in charge of the books for the company and Curt hired our friend, Gary, to be our estimator. We were almost instantaneously busy, filling the schedule with new jobs and building up our clientele. Our home office was eventually too small to keep up with the growth of the company, causing us to move the business to an office building with an attached shop to hold our trucks and equipment.

To be a business owner was stressful, with employees counting on you to keep it running smoothly. Curt handled it all in stride. He definitely had his faults at being the man in charge, and was not perfect at it. You had better believe he was determined, though. With Gary and me by his side, we made a pretty solid team. Gary was in charge of the customer relations, which was never one of Curt's strongest suits. I made sure the books and the finances were in order, and Curt worked with his crews, ordered all materials, and made all of the final decisions. He was incredibly talented with numbers. He could look at a set of architectural plans and instantly find the dimensions of his project, the amount of materials he would need to order, and the time it would take to complete the job.

Curt and Mckenna in one of his American Concrete trucks.

Because Curt had several crews who would be running jobs while he was going to be hunting, he needed to make sure everyone knew the game plan. The materials had been ordered and the crews knew what they needed to do. Of course, Gary and I were available just in case there was an issue, even though there never really had been in years past.

Curt would be gone for a week. He took this bow hunting trip every year at this time, in either July or August. We all knew to expect it because it was something he began planning months in advance, but looked forward to all year long. He even set up his work schedule around the hunting trip so that major jobs were not happening while he was gone. If there was a customer who wanted work done on a complicated job while Curt was hunting, he would refuse. I always admired him for that. He called the shots with his business, and his word was the final word. That was all there was to it. He was very strong and decisive in his thoughts and actions.

Curt's days were filled with preparing his business for his absence, and his evenings were spent with the kids and I. That Monday night, Curt and my mom took Luke and Mckenna to swim lessons while I was in a meeting. Because Luke was so young, either Curt or I had to get into the pool with him each time. Curt always insisted that he be the one to go in the pool with Luke. He wanted to be the one to help Luke learn how to swim. This was so important to him. My mom helped him with Mckenna, getting her in and out of the dressing room, while he swam with Luke. After swim lessons, he brought the kids home, fed them dinner, and got them ready for bed. He was always so proud of himself when he provided such comfort and love for our kids.

We spent our last few days together as a family, not knowing what lay ahead of us. This is a perfect testament to the fact that we don't know what our last moments will look like with our loved ones. I am sure when my family said goodbye to Curt, when leaving Kim and Jon's house, they did not think it would be the last time they would see his face. I know for a fact that when my mom left Curt that Monday night after swim lessons, watching him drive away in his truck, she never imagined it would be the last time she would see him—at least not in this life.

Our days can't be lived in fear of losing someone close to us. They should, however, be lived with the sole purpose of showing our loved ones just how much they mean to us. I am thankful that Curt fully knew the love and admiration that we all had, and still have, for him. Day-to-day living can result in such lethargy in our emotions, leading us to believe that we have plenty of time to express our love for our friends and family. Have you taken the time to really tell your loved ones how much they mean to you? Doing so not because you fear losing them, but because **you really want *them* to walk in *their* life knowing how appreciated and loved they are**? I thank the Lord God every day that He gave me the ability to express this to Curt, so that in his last hours, he knew how deeply he was loved.

Chapter Six

Goodbye to My Love

Forever. What an incredibly powerful word. It means limitless, everlasting, through eternity, an infinite time. It is so clear that it is a word without boundaries. Endless. Yet one dictionary version of the word states, "No one can live forever". So what does this mean? Does this mean that once a person dies, their forever is over? What about two people in love, who have promised each other forever. Is their forever "an infinite time", without limits or boundaries? What if it is time for a person to leave this life, yet their loved ones are not ready to let them go? What if their "forever" isn't over yet?

"We will be together forever, right Amy?"

"Yes, Curt. Forever."

The night before I lost him, this was our conversation. We lay in the dark, in bed, and this was my promise to him. I hadn't even pondered what forever really meant. I just knew that this was my vow to him. It always had been, and always would be. For him, it was a reassurance that our marriage would always last. For me, it was a declaration of my commitment to our life together. A life full of laughter and tears, happiness and sorrow, agreements or not. Raising our children, fulfilling our dreams, planning for our future. We had made it this far. There wasn't an obstacle that we could not climb, a bridge that we could not cross—together.

WEDNESDAY, JULY 30, 2008

The next morning was like every other. Curt got up at about five o'clock and left for work. A good portion of his first hour was spent at Starbucks, talking to anyone and everyone, I am sure. And then he was off to the job sites to make sure everything was running smoothly. After making sure everything was in line for his absence, he made his way home to begin to pack.

At about 11:00 in the morning, I could hear his diesel truck pull up in front of the house. I was on my way out to a meeting for my new position at work, and our nanny, Denise, was getting situated with Mckenna and Luke. I walked out into the garage to find Curt standing there, looking at all the camping gear packed into the shelves he had built along the garage wall. His truck was parked in the street parallel to the house along the curb. A trailer pulling his Rhino (his brand new off road vehicle, purchased just weeks before) was hitched on a trailer to the back of the truck. He had already begun to pack some coolers. This was as close to our conversation as I can remember:

"Hey, Curt! I have to head out to this meeting. So I don't think I will see you again before you leave."

"Ok, honey! I am just loading up the back of my truck (something he found joy in doing, not knowing it was the last time he would). You know what? I am taking the Eddie Bauer tent. Did you realize that it is practically brand new? We only used it one time before we got our trailer. I am not even sure I even remember how to put it up!" he explained.

41

"Yeah, but I am sure once you start setting it up you'll remember." I followed him as he grabbed the tent and walked out to the bed of his truck. He climbed up into it and packed it neatly with the coolers that were already there.

He looked down at me and said, "You know what I have been thinking? The kids need a dog. Every kid needs a dog while they are growing up. Ours are no different. When I get back, I think we should look for one."

"You know," I stated, "it's funny you should say that. I have been looking online at these puppies that are pug and beagle mix. They are called puggles. They're the perfect size, not too small and not too big. They don't grow taller than about your knee. It would be a perfect family dog."

After a minute, I could see Curt's face light up like a light bulb. "How about this?! How about you get a dog, the kids can get a dog, and I'll get a hunting dog?!"

"No!! CURT! We do NOT need three dogs! Are you kidding me? NO! That is ridiculous!" I exclaimed. This was not the first time I had heard of this. About two weeks prior, I received a text from him in the middle of the day that simply stated: *Honey I need a bird dog.* I knew it would not be the last I'd hear about this, either.

I looked up at him and he gave me one of his famous mischievous smiles and said, "We'll talk about it again when I get home." I knew, just from his smile, that somewhere in our future there was going to be a dog. When Curt got something in his mind, he made it happen. If he felt the kids needed a dog, he would find a way to get them a dog. The only thing that worried me was that I was sure he was going to push for at least two. He had been watching shows on television about hunting dogs. This was his forewarning that he was going to start the search. I could feel it.

Curt jumped down from his truck and headed back into the garage. He started gathering some camp chairs when I told him that I really needed to leave for my meeting or I was going to be late. "Denise is in the house with the kids. I already said goodbye to them. They know you are out here getting ready to leave. Oh, and are you going to fix the flat tire on the trailer before you go?" I asked.

In the past day or so, Curt had realized that our camping trailer had acquired a flat tire. He assured me he would have the flat fixed and the trailer moved to our storage unit before he left. "Uh, well . . . about that! You see, I am not going to have time. Work took too long today. So instead, I got you a present so that you wouldn't be mad at me!" He had a look on his face that said, "Isn't that _so_ exciting??"

"Curt! You promised me!! Honestly? I really don't want our trailer sitting out in the driveway for a whole week! Really?"

"I know. I am sorry! BUT, I got you this ipod for your classroom (which he knew I had been wanting so badly) and here is $100. I would like you to go and buy yourself anything you need for your new class."

I have to say I was very impressed that Curt gave me such a thoughtful present, but not at all surprised. He was one of the best gift givers I have ever met. He not only would bring the greatest gifts to me all of the time, but he also found things that I would cherish and love. I already had an idea he was not going to move the trailer before he left. That also was no surprise to me. I had to laugh, even though I was hopeful that he would've taken care of it and a little annoyed that he hadn't.

None the less, standing in the garage, I gave him a long hug and a kiss. We had a quiet moment together, talking about when he would be able to call, and for him to promise to be careful. I thanked him for the gift and told him that I would miss him. I made him promise that he would make sure he was back by the following Wednesday to take Mckenna to her Kindergarten screening. He told me he would, and might be home a bit sooner, depending on when, or if, he got a deer.

And I walked away . . . wishing now I had stood in the garage with him for hours, wishing I had never let him go. He watched me as I climbed into my Jeep Grand Cherokee, parked in the driveway. I closed the door, put on my seatbelt, and started the car. As I began to back out, I stopped and blew him a kiss. He looked right at me, one eye shut in the sunlight, and blew me a kiss back. He smiled at me and then started packing again. And that was it. That was the last time that I saw him. I will forever have those last minutes etched in my mind. They will never leave me. Goodbye to my love.

CHAPTER SEVEN

His Last Night

Once Curt finished packing the back of his truck, he made his way into the house and found his two little loves, Mckenna and Luke. He sat on the couch downstairs with them, each one on a knee, and promised them that he would be back in a week. He hugged and kissed them and told them how much he loved them. He left them with the safe and loving feeling they had always had: when Mommy or Daddy leaves, they always come back. This had always been their truth, so they were satisfied with the fact that he would return in a week from his hunting trip. Mckenna was old enough to remember that he had gone on this trip every year and came back each time, fulfilling this promise.

We all, including our children, are conditioned to believe that nothing bad will ever happen to *us*. We see it on the news, read it in books, or see it in movies, and know that tragedy strikes different people every day. But we put ourselves in our safe little bubbles living with such certainty that our fate will never be matched to theirs. What happens when it is your four year old child learning this lesson with her Daddy as the loss, his tragedy as the lesson to be learned? Looking back and knowing that Mckenna and Luke had no idea it was the last time they would see him makes me so very sad for them. I know they would have held their little arms around his neck so much tighter.

When he pulled away from the house, he drove down the same street he had driven for the past two years, but this time it would be the last. He began the drive towards his resting place, and I had no way of stopping him. I had no way of knowing I should have been stopping him. I imagine he was feeling excited and ready for some much needed rest and relaxation.

From what I understand, he picked up one of his friends, who he had been hunting with every year, and headed out of town. They probably talked about their camping spot, which Curt had scouted two weeks before. They may have discussed how long the journey would be and reminisced of trips in the past. I can only bet that he was relieved to be on this trip finally, after a year of anticipation and preparation.

Curt's first buck bow hunting in August 2007.

At about 1:00, I needed to call Curt about a problem I was having. Our conversation went a little something like this: "Curt, my *Check Engine* light just came on in the jeep. Is it going to be ok if I drive it?" I asked.

He replied, "Yes, I think it will be just fine. It is probably nothing major. If you feel like something is wrong, then take it in. But if it is running ok, just wait and I will fix it when I get home. I'd rather be the one to take care of it for you."

"Alright . . . I will try to wait for you then. Thank you! Are you close to out of town yet?" I asked.

"We are about an hour out right now. So I may lose cell coverage soon. I will call you in the morning once I find where the cell service is up there."

"Ok, Curt—have fun! I love you!"

"We will! Call me if you need anything! I love you too!" he said.

And that was it! Nothing more. Just a simple conversation about a little bit of car trouble. I remember it being something any married couple would say to each other. Just every day life. I hung up knowing that I would hear from him in the morning. Just like every other year that he went hunting. Nothing new. Just a conversation . . . just a conversation . . .

*   *   *

The rest of this part of the story is all hearsay. I was not there. I don't know all of the details. This is what has been explained to me, so this is all I know to tell. When Curt and his friend arrived at their destination, they were about two hours into the back mountain ranges of Humboldt County, Nevada. They instantly took the Rhino (Curt's new prized possession) out for a ride. If Curt was driving, I am sure he was going as fast as the off road vehicle would take them. He loved anything attached to adventure and risk taking. During their ride, they just so happened to get lost and did not find their way back to their camping spot until dark.

Using Curt's truck headlights, they both were able to get their tents set up. Curt had a difficult time remembering how to set up our tent, which he already knew would be a problem. He managed to get the tent pitched and even decided to put the rain flap over the top because he could feel that it was going to be a cold night.

Once they were finished, he and his buddy ate dinner while drinking several beers. When they decided it was time to get to bed, Curt said goodnight and carried his Coleman lantern into his tent with him to go to sleep. I have no idea what his last minutes (or hours) were like. I don't know what he did inside that tent. I don't know what he was thinking. I don't know what he did to prepare for hunting. No one will ever really know.

And that was the last time he was seen alive.

PART TWO

Loss

CHAPTER EIGHT

Twenty-Four Hours Later

THURSDAY, JULY 31, 2008

The night was late. Where had the time slipped away to? The day was gone, it seemed, before it had even begun. I was able to spend the morning with my new students at the park for a meet and greet that I had set up. Afterward, I worked in my classroom preparing for my first week of school. For dinner, my mom and I took the kids to one of our favorite Mexican food hangouts. We talked about our day while the kids played on the restaurant patio. Then we stopped by my parents' house to drop my mom off and spent some time with my dad. Life rolled along as usual, enjoying our time with our family, thankful for the time we had.

Now, back at home, I needed to focus on the next day. I still had a lot to do to prepare. What would the day hold? How would my first staff meeting be at Double Diamond Elementary? New school, new possibilities, new adventures. I was certain that I would love it. What was not to love? I would be closer to home, Mckenna would be attending her Kindergarten class right down the hall from me, and Curt and I just hired a great nanny to watch

Luke while we were at work. I finally felt like I was in the right place at the right time. Everything in our lives was finally falling into place. Finally.

I decided to text him one last time before I went to bed. I hadn't sent him a message since he left because I was sure he was busy with setting up camp, scouting out his areas, and just enjoying himself. It usually took at least a day for him to find a place where he could get service and be able to call me. It was, however, unsettling not to hear from him yet. Stay calm always. There was no need to be worried because why would there be? Everything was always fine. It was always fine. He was always fine, even in tough situations. Not to mention, this was his forte. This was his home away from home. Camping. Hunting. The great outdoors. He was fine.

My text: "Curtis honey—love of my life. Where are you? Why haven't you called me? I miss you so much already. Please call me. Luv amy". There. He would get this text message and know that I was thinking of him. He will see it and smile knowing that we are so happy in our life together. I knew the next day would be so busy and I might not have a chance to text him again. Even after eight years, I couldn't wait to get that call from him, to just hear his voice.

Moving from our bedroom into the bathroom, I walked into our closet to pick out my work clothes for the next day. I knew it needed to be something cute but sophisticated. I found a white button up shirt with tan slacks that would look perfect. Not too dressy, but it showed I am careful of my appearance. I *really* wanted to make a great first impression.

As I began to walk out of the closet, I glanced up at one of Curt's ball caps and it caught my eye. It had blue and white on it. He always looked so handsome in it; I could picture it. He really did always look so handsome in that hat. Suddenly, and without warning, I had such a strange feeling. It took me over, and I was not sure why. What if I looked at that hat again, but when I did, I would be looking at it knowing I would never see him again. What a weird thing to think. Why would someone even think of something like that? I quickly pushed this thought back down into my gut and dismissed it. Of course I would see him again. I'll talk to him tomorrow. He is fine. Why would I even think something like that?

I moved quickly out of our closet to distance myself from the thought. It was late and I was tired. There were plenty of new beginnings tomorrow for me to focus my dreams on tonight. I'll share them with him when he calls in the morning. I climbed into bed, content that the kids were safe and asleep in their rooms, feeling confident and prepared for the next day. As I closed my eyes and drifted off into a deep sleep, I had no idea they were on their way to my house. I had no idea what was in store for me. I had no idea he was already gone.

* * *

What was that? What was that???

I sat straight up in bed cloaked completely in fear. Was that in my dream or did I hear something? What in the *hell* was that? Was that the doorbell!? Yes! It was the doorbell—and then a knock. It was not just a knock; it was a strong, loud knock—like someone was determined to get my attention! Without my glasses on or contacts in, it was hard to see the clock. As I looked closer, I realized that it was midnight. WHY was someone knocking on our door at midnight? Why was this happening with Curt not here to protect us?!! Where was his gun? He probably had it with him! Anything I would need to protect myself and the kids was downstairs. Oh God, help! There it was again!

I reached for the phone noticing that my hands were shaking so much that I could hardly press the buttons to dial.

"Hello?" It was Kim—she sounded as startled as I felt.

"Kim, someone is knocking on my door. They rang the doorbell . . ."

"Ok, here is Jon. It's ok. Here's Jon."

Jon got on the phone and I repeated what was happening. Barely awake he directed me, "Go to Mckenna's window to look down on the driveway and see who it is." I quickly followed his directions. Because I was not in my right mind, I had not even remembered to put on my glasses. As I pulled the blinds open in Mckenna's room, I could barely make out the image of two people standing by my front door. I glanced at Mckenna. Good. She was still asleep. I opened the window and could feel the warm summer breeze through the screen. Jon was still on the phone.

"Hello?" I called out into the night.

Two men moved from my doorstep over to the driveway below me. They directed their question up toward the window where I sat. "Are you Amy Conner?" one of the gentlemen asked.

"Yes, who are you?" I asked terrified. My mind raced. How did they know my name? How did they know my name? If they realized that it was a woman answering at the window and not a man, would they try to break in knowing I am alone? Anyone could see Curt's truck was not in the driveway. His truck was always in the driveway. Oh God, help!!

"We are officers with the Reno Police Department. We need to talk to you. Can you please come and open the door?" one of the men requested.

I spoke into the phone, "Jon, it is Reno PD. They want me to open the door."

Jon instantly replied, "Ok, Amy. It's ok, you can answer it. It is the police. I'll stay on the phone."

But my gut was screaming at me that something was wrong! Terribly wrong! "I can't. I can't! What if it is someone pretending they are the police! I'm scared! How do they know my name?"

I called down to the two men waiting for my response. "How do I know you are police officers? I am not opening the door for you!"

"We understand Mrs. Conner. We will pull our police car in front of your house. We accidentally parked it a few houses down. We couldn't see the street numbers. Hold on. We are going to pull our car in front of your house."

"Jon, they said they are going to pull their police car in front of my house. I don't know why they are here. Why are they here? How do they know my name?"

"It's ok Amy, I am on the phone, so just wait to see the car. You are ok." Jon's gut was screaming at him, too. What was happening?

I could barely make out a police car backing up in the street in front of our house. It looked like a police car. "Jon, they do have a police car. What is happening? Why are they here?"

Jon replied once again, "Amy, they are police officers. It's OK. Answer the door now."

"No, I am not answering the door. Please come here. I am scared. What if they really are not police officers? I don't know what is happening." My whole body was trembling with fear, the kind of trembling that could not be stopped. My stomach felt sick. My legs felt weak. What was happening? What was happening?

"Ok, Amy—I am on my way. Just wait for me to get there. I will be there in a minute. Just wait, ok? Stay on the phone with Kim until I get there."

I called down to the two men—really not sure still if were who they said they were. "My brother-in-law is on his way here. He only lives about a mile away. He will be here in a minute. I just need to know, is everything ok?"

"Everything is ok, Mrs. Conner. We just need to talk to you in person, that is all. And that is great that you have family who lives so close that can come here to be with you. We will wait for him to get here. You just wait right there and we will wait for him. Alright?"

I realized I was still gripping the phone next to my head. I hadn't even remembered it was there. Kim's voice called to me, "Amy, Jon is on his way. What is happening? What is it?" I shook my head. I didn't know. Was Curt in trouble? Had he been in an accident? At the far worst, would he have gotten a DUI while hunting? He would never do that and he was so far out there. That couldn't be the case. Was he in trouble at all? What was it? Was it even about Curt?

"Amy? Are you there? What is it?" Kim asked again.

"I don't know Kim. They said everything is ok. But they know my name. I am so scared. Why are they here? Is he in trouble? Is someone hurt?"

Kim tried to talk me through it. She assured me that everything was fine and Jon was on his way to help me. Honestly she was drowning with fear for me. Trying to allow a million scenarios to pass through her mind, her heart already knew why they were there. We sat in silence and waited for what seemed like an eternity for Jon to get there.

And then something happened. As we waited, I could hear the two men exchanging a conversation—about everyday life—in the driveway below. Something that amused them. One of them began to laugh. They spoke to each other as if there was not even a scared person sitting in the window waiting to hear her fate. Was this just another call to them? This created a fury in me I didn't even realize was there. It erupted into words which I directed toward the driveway. "I am still up here terrified because I don't know why you are here, and you are down there laughing, like nothing is wrong! This is not *funny* to me!" I said in shock. How could they be so insensitive? What about this was amusing to them?

"You're right Mrs. Conner. We are sorry—we are just waiting for your brother-in-law. We will wait over by our police car, ok?" They knew they had offended me. As they moved toward their car, I sat in the window and continued to wait.

And then finally . . . his lights! I could see Jon's lights. "Kim, Jon is here!" I then called out to the strangers, "That is him! That's my brother-in-law!" I quickly left Mckenna's window, but not before looking at her in her bed. The sweet little angel was still sleeping peacefully. Luke was in his bed sleeping, as well. Whatever this was, they did not need to know about. It would scare them to see me speaking to police officers in the middle of the night. I prayed that they stay asleep. I went to my nightstand in our room and grabbed my glasses. With Kim still on the phone, I made my way down the stairs and cautiously unlatched and opened my front door. I slipped into the warm July night in my pajamas, not knowing what was about to be presented to me.

When Jon arrived, he jumped out of his truck and approached the men. The police officers asked him for his ID, which Jon showed to them. I had not yet reached them; nevertheless, they gave him the news first. Curt, his brother-in-law, the man Jon had grown to love like a real brother, had died in an accident. Jon dropped to his knees in the middle of the street. "NO! There are kids up there!" he yelled.

One of the officers pulled him to his feet, sternly telling him to stand up. "You need to get up for her! She is going to need you to be strong!"

Jon looked past their shoulders and saw me coming. Before I reached him, I remember glancing into the back of the police car to see if Curt was sitting in it. A chill passed through my body. He wasn't in the car, making me feel sure this couldn't be about him. It is one of the most haunting feelings I have ever felt. I rushed past the police car and towards Jon, still clutching the phone next to my ear. He looked shaken. He looked at me with eyes that I had never seen before. He was instantly by my side with his arm around me. As he guided me away from his truck, he said, "Oh, Amy—come on inside honey. They need to talk to you." We slowly walked away from his truck, still parked in the middle of the street, policemen following.

An unimaginable fear took over my whole body. Why does he look like that? *What* in the hell is happening?

"Kim, Jon is crying. I don't know what is wrong. We are going inside".

"Just keep me on the phone. Jon is with you . . ."

The next few minutes were a blur to me. As Jon stood by my side in my front room, I received the most devastating news I had ever received in my life. "Mrs. Conner, we are sorry to tell you this, but your husband, Curtis, has passed away. He has died."

"No!!! He is hunting. He is fine. He is **fine**! You have the wrong person! It couldn't be him!" The phone dropped from my hands without my even remembering it was there. My sister sat on the phone and listened as the officer continued. "He died last night. From what we understand from the investigation in Humboldt County, he brought his lantern into his tent with him . . ."

My mind raced. I felt like I was going to throw up. Did the lantern catch his tent on fire?? Please do not tell me that his tent caught on fire.

" . . . and he got carbon monoxide poisoning. The tent was sealed so well that the carbon monoxide from the lantern ate up his oxygen supply. The carbon monoxide got trapped inside. I am sorry Mrs. Conner. He just went to sleep and never woke up. It was an accident," the policeman explained solemnly.

I dropped to my knees and stated that I felt like I was going to throw up. Jon held me while I dropped and said that he felt like he was going to throw up, too. This did not make sense. Where was he? He was ok, right? Where was he? This did not make sense. I was just with him the day before. He blew me a kiss. He is coming home to take Mckenna to her first day of school. How would Reno Police know something like this if he is not even in Reno right now? Is he in Reno right now? Questions, questions, questions.

"Where is he right now?" I demanded.

And the policeman's words that will ring in my mind forever: "He is in a mortuary in Humboldt County." My world spun out of control. A mortuary? By himself?? Was he just in a mortuary by himself? What do you mean? No one was with him? Was he all alone? Was anyone with him? I instantly felt such fear and sadness for him that he was in some building by himself? Where was his hunting buddy? This did not make sense. I needed to be with him! Where was he?

Without my knowing, standing at the banister above the living room, our children sat watching their mother receive the news that their Daddy would not be coming home. "Mommy?" I looked up and saw both of their little faces peering down at me, confused. Their little hands clutched the spindles, their faces pressed in the openings. I instantly pulled myself to my feet and literally grabbed one of the police officers by his uniform and pushed him into the next room where the kids could not see him.

"**NO!** I don't want them to see this! I don't want them to remember this! NO!" And for a split second, I looked into that police officers face and saw such a sad look in his eyes. He was close to tears—because he saw them. He knew. He saw their innocent little faces and knew what we were all about to endure. I will never forget that look in his eyes. It was a connection between two human beings with shared knowledge that death had clutched its cold and uncaring hand around our souls and there was *nothing* I could do to change it.

As I tore up the stairs, two stairs at a time, I realized that Mckenna and Luke were already half way down to me. I scooped them up in my arms and carried them downstairs. I sat on the floor holding them while I wept. The police officers told Jon they would wait outside, in case if we needed them again or had more questions. And they gave him a card. The card had the information of the officers conducting the investigation, the address of the mortuary where Curt's body was being held, and the case number. So concrete to hold on to, yet so surreal and unbelievable to attach case numbers and police officer's names to my husband, Curtis Alan Conner.

I continued to hold on to Mckenna and Luke. I tried to control my sorrow so as not to frighten them. We didn't talk, I just held them. I did not have any idea how the next few minutes, hours, days were going to unfold. What was awaiting our fate? I could only see what was in front of me: Mckenna and Luke. It was now about 1:00 in the morning. The one person who needed to come and put his arms around us was their Daddy, their hero. He was gone! And I didn't even know where he was or how to get to him. God help us! God help him!

CHAPTER NINE

The Longest Night

I looked up from where I was sitting on the floor and saw my sister, Kim, trying to walk in the front door of my house. Once she heard the policeman say those words she had scooped up her two boys, Jake and Ty, out of bed and raced over. The police officers were guarding my door and asked to see her identification. The second she made eye contact with me, though, and I with her—they knew to just let her in. She came to us and dropped to her knees. I do not remember what we said to each other. I was pretty sure Jon was outside with the officers. I only know that I ended up from sitting on the floor by the stairs to up onto our couch in our family room. My two little innocent babies huddled together on my lap, falling quickly back to sleep.

I asked Kim, "Please call Mom and Dad! I need you to call Mom and Dad!"

Kim grabbed my kitchen phone and dialed their number. It rang and rang, but no answer. Kim left a message, "Mom and Dad, it's Kim. Amy is ok! I am at her house. I need you to call us back right away". She looked at me, with Mckenna and Luke now resting on my lap, and asked me if I wanted her to start to call our family.

I remember thinking: Call our family? It is the middle of the night! I was asleep an hour ago and now, at after 1:00 in the morning, we are going to call our family—to tell them what? That Curt had died? I don't even know where he is right now!! What in the hell is happening? What in the hell is happening? I simply replied, "Yes," though, and looked down at Mckenna and Luke, feeling overwhelming grief, confusion, and sorrow.

Kim stood in my downstairs bathroom and made the next call to Julie and Pete. I can only imagine what went through their minds just to hear the phone ring at this hour. It is so confusing and hard to wrap your mind around what could possibly be wrong. Then to hear through the receiver the words, "Curt is dead" must be shockingly and overwhelmingly devastating, beyond what words can describe. Although Kim had whispered the words into the receiver, because she did not want me to hear her say the words, I could hear Pete yelling through the phone from where I was sitting in the other room. A personal chaotic destruction of all of our safe and secure lives was quickly unfolding, and all I could do was sit and watch. There was some murmuring, details being exchanged, something about the lantern. "Get here as quick as you can, please! I have to go, the other line is ringing!"

Kim clicked over to the other line to deliver the heart-wrenching news to my parents that their son-in-law was gone. I know that to my parents this was as close to losing a natural child as you could get. Curt, like all of their son-in-laws, was as close to my parents as they were to their daughters. Our family just has this unique bond that is unbreakable. I worried that my parents may not make it safely to my house because of their inability to drive properly due to grief. How do you drive to your daughter's house knowing the news she just received? My heart still bleeds with sorrow for them for having to watch my pain and suffering, not being able to fix it for me, and having to suffer their own loss and pain at the same time.

Finally, Kim dialed Carrie and Brian's number. Brian answered. "Brian, Curt is dead." Sitting up in bed, Brian loudly repeated, "No! No! No! No! No! No!" over and over. Carrie sat and watched his reaction, still not knowing what was wrong. He asked, "What happened? What happened, Kim?"

"He had an accident. I can't explain it all to you over the phone. It was his lantern. Just get over here as soon as you can!" she pleaded.

Brian hung up the phone in disbelief, explaining to Carrie the news he was just given. His mind instantly felt the same way mine had. Did the lantern burn the tent up? Did he burn to death inside his tent? What in the hell was happening? Carrie found herself on her knees in their hall, where Brian had to tell her to get up and get their precious four week old baby Ashtyn into her car seat. They needed to get to my house as soon as possible. Carrie finally began to move, after repeating, "What is she going to do with those kids without him?" over and over. Disbelief ran through their veins and fear ran through their hearts.

One by one, they all started to walk into my already open front door. I still sat on the couch. Mckenna and Luke were now up and playing with Jake and Ty. Being only two, Luke really had no idea what was happening. At four years old, Mckenna knew something was wrong, but she really did not understand the depth of it all. It was probably confusing for her to grasp that her aunts, uncles, cousins, and grandparents were showing up at our house in their pajamas in the middle of the night. Jake and Ty still had no idea what was happening. All they knew was that they were woken up out of a deep sleep, put into Kim's car and brought to my house. Jake, being the older of the two, was starting to slowly piece it all together, asking Kim if Uncle Curt was alright.

Carrie and Brian were the next to arrive. They had Ashtyn snuggled in her little car seat. Carrie's son, Tanner was with his Dad and did not know of the accident until the following day. Carrie, being my twin sister, has been with me through every single moment of my life. We were born three minutes apart and have been inseparable ever since. When her eyes met mine, we gave each other a look that said, "Oh my God! What are we going to do?" It's been said that twins can hear each other's thoughts and feel each other's pain. There are times in the past when our hearts literally have been able to share each other's hurts. If she is in pain, I can feel it and not even know what is happening. I needed her, now more than ever, to take some of my pain for me. It was more than I could bear. But we both knew she couldn't take this pain away for me.

Julie followed Carrie and Brian in. Pete stayed home with Dylan. By the time she had arrived, which was within ten minutes of her call, I was feeling numb and in disbelief. I had stopped crying, more for Mckenna and Luke's sake than anything, but also because I was in complete and utter shock. Julie had a look of panic on her face, a pure look of fear. She was crying and I remember looking at her and quickly saying, "I don't want to scare the kids." It was also a way of me telling Julie, "I am terrified and I need you to be strong for me. We can't all buckle here. Please!"

Julie, being as close to me as she is, could read this all over my face. With all of the strength she had, she instantly stopped crying and said, "Ok . . . Ok, Amy!" I will never forget that moment and how much it meant to me that she could read what I was feeling and helped me. She probably walked into the next room and sobbed her eyes out. But she never again has given me a look of panic like she felt that night. Nothing but strength from Julie—strength, support, and love, which is all I could ask for.

The last to arrive were my parents. It was probably the hardest thing they had to do—getting ready and driving in their car to come to my house that night. My mom had the same exact look on her face that Julie did, and I said the same thing to her, "Mom, I don't want to scare the kids." My mom didn't even know what to do with this. She couldn't have contained her emotions even if she wanted to. She walked into my kitchen and I could hear her asking questions, trying figure out what was happening, and crying in disbelief. I'm not even going to describe the pain I could feel pouring out of my dad's whole body and soul when he walked into the room. He came over to me while I was sitting on the couch, hugged me, and told me he loved me. He was in such turmoil, beside himself with grief.

For the next five hours, until the sun came up, I can honestly say that I have no idea what we did. I have mentally blocked it. I do know that it was the longest night of my life. It was torture being told Curt was somehow never coming home and then having to wait until daylight when we could get some answers. All of the adults stayed pretty well awake the entire night. Jon and Brian started piecing together a bit of the puzzle. They had to. I was crawling out of my skin trying to figure out what had happened and where he was. I knew he was supposed to be with a few hunting buddies. Where were they? Why hadn't anyone called? Was there anyone who had more information for us? How soon could I get to him?

I was so confused, scared, and sad that he was by himself somewhere. Was somebody there with him? I needed some answers. I needed some damn answers! You don't just come into my house in the middle of the night and then expect me to sit until "office hours" when I could get a hold of somebody who could help me! It was the most frustrated and helpless I had ever or could ever feel in my entire life.

I knew that I did not have a phone number for any of Curt's friends he was hunting with. He had them in his cell phone, but I didn't. After looking in the phone book and searching through some papers, I decided to call our friends, Angela and Gary. It was 2:00 in the morning, and I knew it would be devastating for them to get this call in the middle of the night, but I was hoping they'd have the phone number I was looking for. Reeling from the devastating news, Gary stated that they did not have the number, but he and Angela would be over to the house as soon as they could.

Once they got there, with their baby girl also in her little car seat, I do remember that we all sat on the floor and worked through the details one more time. What was said, I don't know. What was questioned, I don't remember. Did we stare at the wall for much of the time wondering what in the hell was happening? I am pretty sure we did. Did we cry and anguish over Curt's last moments in this life—not having any idea what they actually looked like? Absolutely. Specific details though have escaped my conscious and I am unable to bring them back.

I do know Gary and Angela left after a few hours, and the sun would be up soon. I wanted so desperately to call Curt's family or our closest friends to hear someone on the other line so that I knew this was not just a terrifying nightmare that we were all trapped in. I waited though, much to the request of my mom. She knew that if I would have called Curt's family at three o'clock in the morning, they would have had to do the same exact thing we were doing—sit and wait until they could get some answers. That would be agonizing to know that someone else was suffering the same helplessness that we were feeling.

When I look back on that night, I cannot help but wonder why the police could not have come a few hours sooner? Why wait to wake me up in terror in the middle of the night to deliver this news? Why not come to my house even at nine o'clock when I was still awake? The details slowly began to emerge, little by little. The gut wrenching story began to unfold, piece by piece. Thank God for the daylight . . . and some answers.

CHAPTER TEN

Where is He?

FRIDAY, AUGUST 1, 2008

As soon as the time hit about six o'clock in the morning, I picked up my phone and began to make the calls. I first contacted Curt's family to despairingly deliver this overwhelming news to them. Why would I, at the age of thirty-two, need to be calling family members to let them know their loved one had died? Although I dreaded it, I knew this was my responsibility as Curt's wife—and one of the hardest things I have ever had to do.

I then called my best friend since childhood, Jaimie. This call was one of the most important ones I made that morning. Jaimie and I have been friends since we were two years old. She is by far one of the closest people to me in my life. I needed to have her there with me. I also called Curt's two best friends, also like brothers to him—Chet and Aaron. His family raised Curt for a short time in high school, when Curt lived in San Jose. Aaron was in shock when I explained what had happened and sorrowfully relayed that he and Chet would be on the next plane to Reno. Curt's sister, Misty (whom I love as a sister) said that she would be on a plane to Reno from Los Angeles as soon as she could. Pete and Dylan would also be there soon.

My mom called our close family friend, Linda, who is the secretary of Double Diamond Elementary, to tell her the news. At the time, my sister Kim and my mom also worked at Double Diamond, so this affected three of its staff members. The principal, Dr. Moller, then stood in front of my friends and colleagues in the staff meeting that I was supposed to be in, and delivered the news that my husband had passed away in an accident and that the staff meeting was canceled. I have worked with Dr. Moller for much of my professional career and admire her greatly. I am sure it was as personally difficult to relay this news as it was professionally. I am thankful to her for taking this task for me.

At eight o'clock, we were able to start calling the offices in Humboldt County to find some answers to our heartbreaking questions. After speaking to the police officers who had investigated Curt's death, we came to understand that Curt had died at some point in the night on Wednesday evening. When his friend woke up (from his own tent) the next morning, he tapped on Curt's tent and told him it was time to get up. Curt did not respond, which surprised his friend because Curt was usually one of the first ones up, ready to hunt. After eating breakfast, his friend decided that Curt was obviously too tired to hunt that morning, so he took the Rhino out for a quick ride to give him some time.

Returning to their camp site, Curt's friend realized that he was still not awake. He zipped open Curt's tent to wake him up and made the horrifying realization that Curt was not alive. I can only imagine the fear and the trauma that his friend felt in this moment. He backed out of the tent, jumped on the Rhino and sped off to find help. About one hour into his frantic ride back to town, he came across some workers from the Forest Service. He explained (in so many hysterical words) that Curt had died and he needed help, which sent the Forest Service workers back the rest of the way to town to call the police.

I spoke to the officer who actually led the investigation at the scene. He explained that when he got there, the only conclusion he was able to make is that the carbon monoxide from the lantern poisoned Curt's system. He knew for a fact by looking at Curt that it was a result of carbon monoxide, but he would not know if there were any other contributing factors until the autopsy report came back. I asked him, "Is there anything that I need to know. Is there anything that he could have done to prevent this or helped himself?"

He said this to me: "Amy, it was an accident. It was purely an accident that he could not have helped because he didn't know it was happening. Carbon monoxide is a silent killer. He could not smell it, taste it, or see it. He had no idea it was slowly killing him. I investigated every inch of that tent. There was no air flow. The tent was so well sealed, especially with the rain flap on it. The air, mixed with the carbon monoxide, was trapped inside and there was nothing he could have done unless he knew it. Honestly Amy, he just fell asleep and never woke up."

I asked him why I had not been contacted until Thursday at midnight if Curt had died on Wednesday night. This means that Curt was out there, with police officers investigating his death for an entire day, while I ran my errands and went to dinner—not having any idea that my husband was gone! He explained, "by the time Curt's friend found him, was able to get help, we (the police) got back out to them, conducted our investigation, and got Curt back into town, it had been a full twelve hours. He was so far back in the mountains that we couldn't even get an ambulance to him. We had to bring Curt's body to town in the back of our truck. We then had to call the Reno Police Department, they had to find your address and information, and dispatch two police officers to your house to give you the news. This was the reason it took so long to get back to you. Until they concluded their investigation, it was not possible to inform you of his passing."

The lantern, he said, had been sent to a lab to be tested. They wanted to make sure that it was not defective and did not have any leaks in it. He would call me when the results of that report were submitted to him. He also let me know that Curt's body was being held at the mortuary in Humboldt County. This made me sick to my stomach. I could not process all of this information. I hadn't heard from his friend and I had no idea who was with him. My family could tell I was panicking in a massive way. When were they bringing him home? Why was he alone? Could I go there to be with him? What was happening? Jon and Brian finally looked at me and said, "Amy, you say the word and we will go to Humboldt County to be with him. If they can't get him home until tomorrow, we will stay the night and wait for when they are ready."

It took me half of a second to decide. Before I could say, "Yes, *please*!" they were gone! My mom handed them the keys to her car because theirs were all blocked in. They were on the road to be with Curt within minutes, which helped me calm my panic. It was explained to us that there were no plans to even bring him home to Reno until the next day. The mortuary simply did not have time to get him back to us or the proper vehicles. However, Pete was able to talk them into rearranging their schedule to get him home that day. If there was one thing that I could not have been more thankful for it was for my brother-in-laws. Between the three of them, they managed to get my husband home and be by his side through the process. 'Eternal gratitude' are the only two words I can think to describe my feelings for them.

I found myself feeling overwhelmed and needing some space. I stood up from the couch I was lying on and walked out my front door. I walked across the grass and glanced over at the camping trailer sitting in the driveway. Damn trailer. If he had just taken it, this would not be happening. I kept walking until I reached the front curb where I sat down, feeling the morning sunlight on my skin. I was still in my pajamas from the night before, but I could have cared less what I looked like. I put my head down on my arms and cried.

After about ten minutes, I heard a car pull up in front of the house. It was Linda, bringing some food for the people who had already arrived. She left school after the staff meeting to come and see if there was anything I needed. She sat down on the curb next to me. I remember our conversation so clearly. I have known Linda since I was two years old. Her family lived across the street from ours throughout my entire childhood. With my face still resting on my arms, I said, "He's gone. He was here and now he is gone. What am I going to do?"

Linda said to me, "Amy, you are going to be strong. You have a family who will take care of you and help you and you will take care of those babies the best way you know how."

I pulled my head up with a tear stained face and said, "Linda, you know how people say sometimes that their heart hurts? You know, like from a broken heart? My heart really and truly hurts right now. It hurts me right now. It hurts me to breathe. I don't know how I am going to do this." Linda put her arms around me and told me that everyone would be here to help me. She knew I had strength and would do what it took to survive this. She hugged me, and knowing I needed some more time, stood up and took the food inside to my family.

About ten minutes later, the next car pulled up, and in it was my good friend Trish. She is the school counselor at Double Diamond and I had worked with her in a previous school for years. She had an idea of what I was feeling because she lost her husband at a young age, as well. When she sat down next to me, I knew she had felt before what I was now feeling. I remember saying to her, "So now what, Trish, so now I'm just a widow?"

To which she said, "No Amy, you are not *just* a widow. You are a mother and a sister and a daughter and a friend and a teacher. This is not going to be who you are, Amy. You will do the best that you can, and it is going to be the hardest thing you have had to do. But it is not who you are." I knew in the back of my mind she was right, but I had a hard time convincing myself of it. The past eight years of my life had been dedicated to being a good wife and mother. I loved being married to Curt and taking care of our kids. I felt like I didn't know who I was now. I felt terrified and alone.

I stood up from the curb with Trish and walked into the house. My sisters and I decided it was time to explain to the kids what was happening. Trish was going to help us with this process, which I was so thankful for. We called Mckenna, Luke, Dylan, Ty, and Jake into my front room, the same place that I had received the news the night before. We sat them down on the carpet and I said to them, "I have something that I need to tell you. Mckenna and Luke, your Daddy is not going to be able to come home from his hunting trip. I learned last night that he has died." Five little faces just stared at me. Nothing. No response at all. "When he went to sleep, he breathed in some bad air from his lantern and it made him stop breathing. He won't be coming home at all. He is in Heaven now." Still nothing. I don't know if they just were too young to understand or if they were in shock, but they all just stared at me. "Does anyone have any questions for me or do you even understand?"

Jake, being the oldest of the kids in the room, asked, "Is that why the policemen were here last night?" I explained that it was and that they told me that he had died the night before. I looked into Mckenna and Luke's tiny little faces and it was as if they didn't understand what was happening. They really did not know what this meant. Kind of as if they wanted to say, "Ok, but when is he coming home?"

I personally felt like it was all too much for them to take in. The midnight wake up, the police, the people, and the tears. As a child, I believe you just want to revert to any normalcy you can, which is play. So that is what I sent them back to do. There is a quote that I found written by an anonymous author that says, 'Play is the child's main business in life; through play he learns the skills to survive and finds some pattern in the confusing world into which he was born.' During these first few days, this is what our kids learned to do—play to find a sane pattern in all of the grief that surrounded them.

About an hour later, another of Curt's nephews was about to learn of his Uncle's death. Tanner, arriving home from a visit with his Dad, was picked up at the airport by Pete. Pete said nothing to him about what had happened during their car ride to my house. When they pulled up to the house, he noticed all of the cars parked in front and knew something was wrong. As he approached the house, he saw his mom Carrie, Julie, Kim, and my dad standing in the garage. They all were clearly shaken, something any nine year old would be able to see. Carrie sat him down on Curt's workout bench and told him she needed to talk to him.

"Tanner, something happened to your Uncle Curt while he was hunting. He had an accident."

"*Okay*, is he alright?" Tanner replied.

"No Tanner, he is not alright. Honey, in his accident, your Uncle Curt died."

My sisters have all said that the look on Tanner's face that day will always haunt them. They have said that words cannot really describe the way he looked at them when they told him the devastating news. Tanner was the oldest cousin and had spent the most time with Curt. They had been bonded with each other since Tanner was two years old. Nothing could have prepared Tanner for the shock he felt that day. Unlike most of the other kids, he was old enough to know what this meant. The indescribable pain and utter disbelief on his face was probably nothing close to what he felt in his heart. What an agonizing loss for a young boy to cope with. He found me within minutes and since that morning has done everything his Uncle Curt would want him to do to help me in this life. I know his uncle is so proud of him.

*   *   *

It took Jon and Brian two hours to get to Winnemucca. Upon arriving at the sheriff's department, they were informed that the vehicle that held Curt's body in it was a white van (because this was the only thing they had available). It had just left ten minutes prior. The sheriff was not supposed to be giving them this information, but the van had a dent in the right back fender and they needed to leave right away if they were going to catch it. I am certain, after being up all night and as upset as they were, that they were emotionally and physically exhausted. To drive two hours and then turn around to try and find the van Curt was in had to be maddening.

After driving well past the speed limit, they were able to catch the white van. It is hard to imagine what they were feeling when they saw it. I don't know that I can fathom what was going through their minds. They went from learning of Curt's death to escorting his body home, which had to have been unreal—beyond what words could describe.

My house phone rang and it was Jon. The news was passed to me. "They are behind the car that is bringing Curt home. He is not alone anymore, Amy. They are with him." I sat down and cried. I cried for Curt, and our children, and our family. I cried for Pete having to make such a desperate call. I cried for Jon and Brian having to make such a desperate drive. I cried for the fatigue that I felt and for the strength I knew I needed to have. And I cried because all I really wanted was for Curt to put his arms around me and take it all away. He couldn't take this away for me. What do you do, as a mother and as a wife, when you are left with the cross of it all to bear?

Curt, Jon, and Brian at a Kenny Chesney concert in July of 2007.

CHAPTER ELEVEN

Empty Answers

A few hours later we received another call that Curt was now back in Reno. Jon and Brian needed me to meet them at the Coroner's office in downtown Reno. Chet and Aaron, who had arrived a few hours earlier, drove me to meet them. We pulled up to the Coroner's office and I could see my mom's car parked in the parking lot. I knew now that this was the right place, even though I had never been there before. There was a Hurst parked in the back of the building, and I wondered if it was there because of Curt. I knew very few details. As we walked up the front steps, I could see Jon and Brian waiting outside the front door for us. They looked exhausted and heartbroken.

After hugging them, I asked them, "Is Curt here right now?"

They let me know that he was there, and that they had followed the van he was in to this building. The coroner was inside waiting to talk to me. They wanted to know if I was ready, and I told them that I was. To be perfectly honest, I did not know what they were going to tell me. This was as close as I had gotten to Curt since the day I left him in the garage. I was not sure, but I thought I was about to be standing in the same building as him. Were they going to let me see him? Was I going to receive more information about his death? The only thing I was sure of is that I was extremely confused and exhausted.

We entered through the front doors and were ushered into a room to the right. The room was filled from wall to wall with windows which brought a lot of light into it. In the middle, there was a long conference table surrounded by chairs. The coroner followed us into the room and closed the door. He introduced himself to us. I felt weak and empty in my soul, not sure if I could handle what he had to tell me.

After explaining that Curt had arrived here at the Coroner's office from Humboldt County, I immediately asked him, "Can I see him?"

He looked at me sadly and said, "No, we are not going to let you see him. You don't want to see him, Amy."

"But why? Have *you* seen him? Why can't I see him?" I pleaded. At this point in time, I am not sure what I would have done if he had said that I could see him. I knew nothing about what he may look like or how I might have reacted. I just needed to know if they would let me.

"Amy, I have seen your husband, and I am telling you that we are not going to let you see him. The condition of his body is past a point where you would be allowed to see him. I am so sorry."

"What do you mean, 'the condition of his body'? Doesn't he look just like he would if he had just passed away?" I honestly felt like I was going to throw up! I looked around and saw Jon and Brian, Chet and Aaron. I saw the looks on their faces, and the sadness that they felt.

The coroner looked at them first and then to me. He responded, "No, Amy, he does not look the same. You don't want to see him, Amy. Not like this."

"Where is he right now? Where is he *in this building* right now?" I asked frantically.

The coroner responded, "He is in a room right below us right now." He pointed below where we were standing.

"Can I at least stand outside of the door to the room he is in? I just want to be as close to him as I possibly can. I need to be close to him, so he knows I am here."

"I am so sorry, but you cannot go downstairs to stand outside the door. It is prohibited. Right here in this room is as close to him as you are going to get."

I started to cry, knowing that this man was not going to budge on allowing me to be near Curt. I felt like losing my mind. I felt like throwing punches and pushing people over to get to the room Curt was in. I was not thinking of having to see a body that was in a poor condition. I was thinking only of finding my husband and letting him know that I was there and everything was going to be ok.

Knowing there was not much more that he could do for me at this time, the coroner said, "I do have this envelope for you." He pulled out the contents of the envelope and put them on the table. "In it are Curt's wedding ring and his Leatherman pocketknife that he had on his belt at the time of his death". I stared in disbelief at the two items on the table and picked up the ring. It was *his* ring. Curt's wedding ring. The ring I put on his finger the day we promised to spend our lives together. His wedding ring. I knew in this moment that he was really gone. Oh my God, he was really gone! They didn't have the wrong person! It wasn't all a mistake. It was Curt's wedding ring. It was his ring. He was really gone! He was really gone! He was really gone!

I put Curt's Leatherman back into the envelope and held onto the ring. I was asked if I wanted a moment to myself, in which I weakly said 'yes'. Everyone agreed to give me some time while they waited outside of the room. One by one they hugged me and walked out the door. As soon as the door shut, I dropped to my knees, laid myself down on the floor, and sobbed. If they weren't going to let me anywhere near him, I was going to get as close to him as I could, and this was the only way I knew how.

I lay with my face pressed to the carpet and spoke towards the floor below me, "Curtis, I am so sorry. They won't let me near you. I need you to know I am here. I have your ring. I don't know what is happening right now. I am so scared and I need you. I love you and I am so sorry that I cannot help you right now."

And then I lay there in silence, sobbing into the floor, hoping my tears would reach him. Hoping he could feel the love and longing I felt for him through the floor. I didn't want to move. I didn't want to leave him. I didn't want him to be alone.

After what seemed like forever, I literally peeled myself up off of the floor, clutching his ring in my hand, and forced myself to open the door to the office. Four of Curt's closest friends stood solemnly outside waiting for me.

As I walked through the parking lot back to the car, I took my wedding ring and diamond band off, put Curt's ring on my finger, and replaced my two rings. Now our rings were together and safe where I could have them with me at all times. I stopped and looked back towards the building where Curt lay. I didn't want to leave. I didn't want to leave him there. I didn't want him to be alone. I knew now that it was him, even though I never was allowed to see him. I had to take everyone's word for it that my husband was there in that building. I came to get answers and left feeling emptier than I had when I arrived.

While it comforted me that he was at least home—not in another county, I was overwhelmed with feelings of helplessness.

Now what? Where did we go from here? Where in the hell did we go from here?

*   *   *

Sitting in my living room, leaning forward with my arms resting on my knees, I knew my sisters, my mom, and my friends were worried for me. It was now about 11:30 pm and I had not eaten in over twenty-four hours. My last meal was the one I had at the Mexican food restaurant with my mom the night before. The thought of food now made my stomach hurt. I knew it would be better for me to eat, but I wanted nothing to do with it. Julie brought me a piece of toast and some juice. I looked around to all of the exhausted faces hoping they could get me to eat even a bite of it. I explained that I simply was not hungry and pushed the plate away from me. I could barely keep my eyes open, but the thought of going to sleep terrified me.

Knowing I would have to wake up in the morning to relive this nightmare was more than I could handle. If I just stayed awake, maybe something would change. Maybe Curt would walk in the door and everyone could go home. Maybe someone would call and say it was all a mistake. Maybe this was all really just a nightmare and I would wake up. Maybe, maybe . . . .

Julie turned to me and said, "Amy, I know that you do not want to eat, but you have got to get something in your stomach. This is not good for you to go this long without any food. Can you please eat just a bite of the toast?" I couldn't even respond. It was as if I could not speak. I just shook my head and lay down on the couch. It was no use trying. I felt like there was no part of me that could even function. As I lay there, I remember feeling so desperately lost and alone. Knowing that you yearn for someone so badly but cannot have them creates an abyss inside your soul. The abyss can't be reached or filled or repaired. It is just a quiet, lonely black hole in your soul that a person has to endure because there is no choice. That is how I felt laying on that couch. I wanted to accept everyone's help, but this abyss had taken over my being and nothing else mattered.

At about midnight, after agreeing to take a sleeping pill (which I had never done before), I started to doze off. I agreed only to go to sleep as long as I did not have to sleep alone. My sisters helped me up to my room to lie down. I had not been in this bed since the police knocked on my door the night before. I climbed up into it and lay down in between Mckenna and Luke, who had already been long asleep. All three of my sisters lay down on an inflatable mattress that sat on the floor at the foot of my bed. I was in oblivion to all that was happening.

I fell into a deep sleep within seconds only to be awoken about ten minutes later. Without any warning I sat up and felt like I was going to be sick. I scrambled out of my bed and made it just in time to the bathroom. I hardly remembering this happening, but of course, my sisters were all there to help me through this and, in time, back into my bed. I was emotionally and physically in distress. My body needed me to sleep to help me battle all of these emotions.

I wearily lay back down in the middle of the two kids, on my stomach, with my arms wrapped around each one. I just needed to feel them both close to me. I felt such grief for them knowing that they had no idea what all of this really meant. The three of us lay there that night in mine and Curt's bed, the scent of him still on our pillows. I fell asleep aching for him, wondering when this nightmare was all going to end.

At some point during that desperate night, the most astonishing thing happened. I remember so vividly that a sudden calm fell over my entire body. It was as if I felt Curt's body laying over the three of us, his arms covering mine. I could feel the four of us lying together, one last time as a complete family, Curt there to comfort and protect us. I did not want to even move, praying that he wouldn't go away. It was the most peaceful feeling I had felt since learning of his death. I had never felt Curt's soul that clearly, even during his life. It was unmistakable that he came to us that night, but as in his life, he could only stay for so long.

When I woke in the morning, I opened my eyes and realized he was gone.

CHAPTER TWELVE

Letters to Heaven

Making my way downstairs the next morning, I found at least twenty people walking around my house. Every member of my family was there. Chet and Aaron, who slept on my couches, were in the kitchen, and five or six of my friends were there to check on me. Brian's parents, Nancy and Harry, had just arrived from California to take care of Carrie and Brian's four week old baby girl, Ashtyn. I am so thankful for the blessings Harry and Nancy have brought to my life and the love that they have shown our family. I was also thankful that all of these people were there in my house with me, and at the same time I felt like I stranger in my own home. Seeing everyone made it so much more real that Curt was not coming home.

I glanced into the backyard and noticed that our good friend Jeff was standing there with one of my sisters. I opened the slider and joined them on the patio. He and Curt worked together on a daily basis. His landscape company, Sierra Nevada Landscapes, referred Curt business for patios and foundations—and Curt did the same for him with landscaping projects. This was the first time I'd seen Jeff since learning of Curt's death. He hugged me, tears in his eyes, and asked me if there was anything I needed. I told him that I was going to go crazy sitting inside my house. Could he please help me fix the backyard up so that I could sit out there and enjoy the patio, fire pit, fountain, and landscape that Curt had taken such care in building? Within hours, Jeff had several people working on my backyard—pulling weeds, planting flowers, mowing the lawn, and making sure the fountain was working properly. Curt was so proud to call Jeff a friend, and to this day . . . so am I.

Inside the house, Brian and Jon were getting ready to leave. They had received the call that Curt's truck was now in Reno. Once the Humboldt police finished their investigation and brought Curt into the Humboldt County Coroner's Office, they allowed his friend to pack up all of his camping gear back into his truck to bring home to me. Brian and Jon were on their way to pick it up. This was another bridge we were going to need to cross—and I was ready for it. Not having him or his truck here was more than I could take. I was being told that he was gone and yet didn't have anything of his to hold onto.

I stepped back inside and walked back upstairs to my room to get dressed. I still hadn't eaten anything and was feeling weak, but the thought of eating made my stomach hurt. As I passed my nightstand, a picture of Curt and I caught my eye. Picking up the frame, I stared at it in disbelief. He was so full of life and happy. Where was he now? Where was this man that I had built this life with? I dropped to my knees and began to sob.

I felt in my heart that I was losing myself in this downward spiral of grief. I needed to talk to him. I didn't know where he was. I didn't know if he was watching me or if he was in a different dimension and could not see what I was going through. He had been my husband, confidant, and best friend for eight years now.

I wanted to call him on the phone and ask him, "Curt, what do you want me to do about this? All of these people are in our house and I don't know what to tell them! You'll be home in a week, so they don't all need to stay and worry, right?" I was sure that at any moment, my cell phone would ring and it would be Curt and he would reassure me that this all was a terrible mistake.

Sitting on my floor in my bedroom, I knew that there had to be a way for me to talk to him. I tried to speak out loud to him, and I felt like I was losing my mind! Where was I directing my words to? Where was he? Could he hear me? Was he sitting next to me? Was he watching me suffer? Could he feel the enormous pain pulsing through my entire body and soul?

As I contemplated these questions, something caught my eye. There, sitting on the floor of my room was a pile of books and papers that I had bought for my new job. In the middle of that pile was a brand new journal. It was full of fresh sheets of lined paper, the type of notebook used in a college course. There were about two hundred sheets waiting to be filled with everything I had to say to my husband and didn't know how to. As plain as day, I knew this would be the way I would connect with him.

I have always written in journals, especially in difficult times in my life. I know this is a cathartic method to unleashing emotions instead of keeping them bottled up inside. I didn't want to write how I was feeling, though. I wanted to write my thoughts to Curt so that if he were able to see me doing this, he could read them while I wrote. In all of this madness of the past twenty-four hours, the only thing I desperately needed was a means of communicating my thoughts to him.

Moving to my hands and knees, I crawled over to the pile and grabbed the journal. Then I stood up, walked to my nightstand, found a pen in the top drawer, and headed downstairs. I walked past several people standing in my kitchen and out to the garage. There was a new tension in the air, knowing that Curt's truck was about to arrive. I knew my friends and family were watching my actions to make sure I was alright and mentally prepared for this event to transpire.

I walked over to the radio that was plugged in on Curt's workbench. Sitting in the CD player was a disc that I had made for Curt a few weeks before. It was filled with a playlist of all of the songs that reminded me of him. He was so thankful that I made this little gift for him. While he worked in the garage, he played it on this radio . . . and here it still sat in the CD player.

Starting the music, I sat down on some workout equipment, opened the journal, and began to write:

> *Curtis—I don't even know what day it is. I think it is Sunday. The past few days have been a blur. I am sitting in the garage right now, listening to the CD I made for you. I just listened to "Stealing Cinderella"* (his favorite song that reminded him of Mckenna), *which could probably bring me to my knees every time I hear it. Right now it is Kenny Chesney, "There Goes My Life". Luke is with me and we are on the Bowflex. He is sitting on my lap. He found one of your hunting elk calls and keeps blowing it. It is so ironic because we are sitting here waiting for Jon and Brian to bring me your truck.*
>
> *I am listening to "Hero" now* (our wedding song). *You know, it says, "I just want to hold you"—and you know Curt, I just want to hold you. I just want to hold you. I just want to hold you.*

Carrie just told me that it is Saturday. I didn't think it was really Sunday. It just seems like forever ago that the policemen came to our house. They woke me up out of my sleep and I was so scared. I was shaking and crying because I didn't know who it was.

I stopped writing. I could hear it . . . the sound of Curt's truck. It was unmistakable to me because I had heard it so many times before. I set Luke on the ground next to me, let go of my journal, and stood up. My dad was next to me within seconds. I looked at the cross street leading to my house, and there it was. His big, beautiful, strong, white Dodge Ram truck. I felt a wave of nausea run through my body. Jon was driving it and slowly turned in front of my house.

There it was—he took so much pride in that truck. Jon parked it in the same exact spot Curt had when he was loading it up to leave. Now, three days later, it was back and he was not in it. I stood at the top of the driveway, watching as Jon and Brian solemnly stepped out of the truck. They both walked to me and hugged me. Then they left me to approach the truck by myself and have some time to process what was happening. My parents, sisters, and brother-in-laws stood at the top of the driveway while I made my way towards it.

I walked around to the driver's side, opened the door, and pulled myself up into the seat. I looked around, trying not to overload myself with all that was here to be found. His sunglasses hung from a case hooked onto the lighter. In the center console sat his cellular phone. I picked it up, knowing that his hands were the last to hold this phone. I held it to my forehead and sighed. Pushing the power button, a new message instantly appeared. I clicked on it, wondering who had possibly sent him a message. My heart sank and I began to cry.

It said, "Curtis-honey, love of my life. Where are you? I haven't heard from you yet. I miss you so much already! Please call. love amy"

Damnit!! I wanted to throw the phone through the windshield! It was the message I sent to him that he never got. When I sent it, he was already gone and I had no idea! This was an excruciatingly painful realization to have had to make!

I looked around at the inside of the truck. Curt spent hours and hours in this truck, making it his own. His seats even had camouflage seat covers on them. He was everywhere I looked. I sat for a minute with my head back, trying to take it all in. In the back seat sat all of Curt's camping totes—the ones he packed just days before in the garage. They were filled with his clothes, hunting gear, and camping supplies. I opened one and began to cry. It was painfully evident that he packed each tote with such thought and care. He was prepared to enjoy a week of hunting with his buddies. He had no idea he would not make it past the first night.

I snapped the lid shut and felt a little hand on my knee. Luke, climbing into the truck next to me, pulled himself up and sat on my lap. He grabbed onto the steering wheel and pretended to drive his Daddy's truck. He was too little to understand. As he climbed through the truck and started to explore, I saw my dad approaching. He opened the passenger door and looked at me as if he wished he could take away the sorrow written all over my face. He looked through the truck with me, talking about different memories and making sure everything was in its place.

The one thing that I couldn't find was Curt's wallet. His phone was sitting in the console, so why was his wallet not there?

I wanted to look at his driver's license. I wanted to make sure everything was there. I voiced my concern to my dad, and within minutes one of my brothers was on the phone with the sheriff's office to get some answers. It appeared that Curt's friend gave it to the detectives so that he did not have it in his possession. He was trying to be safe with it and all of its contents. The only problem was that the sheriff's department was not going to release it to me until their investigation was complete. At this point I could expect to receive it in the mail. It seemed like everything was coming to me in bits and pieces. I was grateful to have Curt home and now his truck, but I felt much anxiety about not having his wallet, too. It was something he carried on him every day of his life and now it was gone.

Jon and Brian informed me that they first took Curt's truck to his shop to look through it and make sure there was nothing that would upset me. Inside the back of the truck was the tent that Curt had passed away in. They opened it up and searched it to see if there was anything in it that was his that may have been left behind. The only thing they found was some of Curt's chapstick which was in a side pocket. Jon handed it to me, and I took it in disbelief. How could something so simple bring me such relief to have? Curt always had chapstick on him, everywhere he went. He probably used this the night he died. I tucked it appreciatively into my pocket. Brian and Jon explained that once the tent was empty, they threw it in the trash. They thought it would be too hard for me to see it and knew I would never use it again. So it was gone and I was relieved to have not had to see it. I made way inside the house to gather my thoughts.

Back inside the house, I sat down on the couch and stared at the wall in front of me. I was on overload. The pain in my heart was getting worse and worse by the minute. I still hadn't had anything to eat. My sister Julie sat down next to me and said, "Amy, what can I do? If there is one thing that you would need right now, what would it be? Do you want to talk to anyone? Do you need anything?"

"I need to talk to Kimie." Kimie is one of my greatest friends. I taught with her, sharing a contract, just before I moved to my new teaching position. She had already been to the house the previous day to help me, but the only thing that was going to make me feel better at that point was to talk to her again. Julie dialed her number and handed me the phone. Kimie talked to me for a few minutes and then told me she would be over as soon as she could. She wanted to know if there was anything that I needed. Was I hungry yet? Not having eaten in two days, I told her the only thing that I was sort of wanting was a Peach Carrot Twist juice drink from Keva Juice. She said she would be right there with it.

When Kimie got there, I tasted the drink that she brought to me and felt relieved to have found something that I could put into my empty stomach. For the next week straight, Kimie came to my house with a Peach Carrot Twist, sometimes twice a day. It was the only thing I drank (or ate) because it was the only thing I could think of that I wanted; nothing else sounded good. Kimie's support was *much* more than this though, and I am so thankful that she is my friend.

Misty arrived a few hours later, and I felt a sense of relief. Misty is Curt's step-sister, but I consider her far closer than that. We share a very special bond. A few weeks before Curt died (while he was scouting his hunting spot in Humboldt County) I was in Los Angeles with the kids visiting Misty, her husband Gary, and their three kids. Now two weeks later, here she was arriving at my house in distress that her brother was gone. We sat down on the couch to talk. After a little while, feeling lost in all of my emotions, I remember just staring ahead at the blank TV, not able to speak.

Luke was asleep on my lap, which was not a surprise to anyone. He followed me everywhere I went. During these days Mckenna was much more independent with all of the kids and people in our house, but Luke was just the opposite. He was worried and just wanted his mommy with him at all times. The only person he left the house with was my dear friend, Lori. He wouldn't leave with anyone else other than family. So there he lay on my lap, his Mommy lost in anguished thought. After a while, Misty walked up to me, put her hand on my shoulder, and said, "Amy, maybe you should get up and walk around. It would be good to stretch your legs, don't you think?"

I said, "Why? I'm fine where I am. I don't want to get up."

She replied, "Amy, honey, you have been sitting in that exact same position staring at that blank TV for the last four hours. I think you need to get up and move around. OK?" Four hours? Really? Was she sure? I don't remember sitting there for four hours, but my mind had escaped into another dimension—probably reliving Meeks Bay the weekend before, or the conversation with the police that night, or my last minutes spent with Curt in the garage.

I agreed to stand up, with Luke toddling right behind me, making my way into the kitchen. An entire group of friends and family were there preparing dishes and refreshments for all of the company in the house. I remember my mom walking up to me and asking, "Do you think Amy will want lasagna for dinner?" It was the first time my mom had honestly confused Carrie and I as twins since I could remember. In the chaos of these first few days, her mind (like all of ours) was not in its right place.

I looked at her and said, "Yes, Mom, I think she would want lasagna for dinner." As my mom agreed and walked aimlessly out of the kitchen, Carrie walked in. Two of our friends were having a quiet conversation about the road construction that had delayed one of their arrivals to my house. Apparently the traffic on the freeway was backed up for miles. While our two friends continued their conversation, I looked at Carrie with a feeling that life should not keep moving forward. Doesn't everyone in the world know that my husband has died? Carrie looked at me, knowing what I was thinking. To confirm our thoughts, I said to her, "And life goes on . . ." because it does. The world does not stop spinning for your pain and suffering. Life outside of your tragedy is still life. There is nothing that we can do to stop it. Nothing.

By then end of the night, I was mentally and physically exhausted! I willingly crawled into my bed, next to Mckenna and Luke, knowing I needed to rest. The next day was going to be a long one, and I needed to be able to survive it. Finding my journal to Curt sitting at the edge of my bed, I opened it and began to write:

> *I just read that last journal to you and I realize that I didn't even finish it. At that exact same moment, your truck pulled up and I just dropped the journal. I could hear your truck coming and knew it was yours. Oh—the feeling of knowing you weren't in it was enough to break my heart into a million pieces. Your truck is so big and bold and you—and you were not in it. But at least I had it back and that was all that mattered. It was so incredibly hard to know you were not in Reno, and your truck was not in Reno—and finally I have you both back. I looked in your truck, and Luke climbed right in. To see your seatcovers, and your sunglasses hanging from*

the lighter, your bow and arrow cases and hunting/
camping gear—made it so real for me. Like you
were really not coming home. Oh, baby—why?
What happened? I have to go to bed now Curtis. I
can barely keep my eyes open! It is midnight and I
am totally wiped out. Until the morning! I hope you
stay near me tonight. I love you with all of my heart
and miss you more than you will ever know. I love
you! I love you! I love you!

~Love Your Wife

I fell asleep that night knowing that I would be meeting with the funeral director the following morning. I would be going with my parents to make Curt's funeral arrangements. Once again, I had no idea what this meant. I had never even stepped inside a funeral home, and now I would be going to arrange Curt's funeral. It's a confusing and terrifying feeling to have to fall asleep to. I was beyond exhausted, though. Lying down in my bed, next to my sleeping babies, I could hear different people milling around my house. Someone was doing the dishes, someone was doing a load of laundry, others were talking quietly in the front room. I couldn't keep track of who was where. I only knew that I was in my bed wishing Curt was lying next to me, kissing my face goodnight . . . .

Chapter Thirteen

The Arrangements

SUNDAY, AUGUST 3, 2008

The following morning, my parents came to pick me up at my house. I knew the kids were in great hands. There were so many people in my house, and I knew one of my sisters had them. I slowly made my way down the stairs and out the front door. Climbing into my parents' car, I thought to myself, "What now? Why are we going here? To make funeral arrangements? What does that mean?" In my mind, I really did not comprehend what we were about to do. It was the same helpless feeling I had going to the Coroner's office. Nobody gives you a handout or a pamphlet on the process of losing someone. You just go where you are told you need to go and prepare yourself as best as you can.

When we walked into the front doors, a gentleman escorted us to a waiting room. The funeral director would be meeting us here. I sat down, not knowing what to expect. My parents sat next to me, feeling the same grief I was feeling. The funeral director joined us and offered his condolences. He explained that he was going to need to ask some questions to complete the application for the death certificate. He asked me all sorts of questions including Curt's date of birth, his social security number, and his birthplace.

At one point he asked me what Curt's ethnicity was and I began to laugh in the middle of my tears. Curt's heritage came from a mix of Spanish and Italian. Every year when it was Cinco de Mayo, he would say to all of his friends and family, "So, are we going to celebrate the heritage of my people?" Then, when the Italian festival would come to town, he would say, "We need to go so we can celebrate the heritage of my people!" And because his last name was Conner, he felt that meant he had a little bit of Irish in him (which he did not). So on St. Patrick's Day, he would say, "I hope you all wore green so you can celebrate the heritage of my people!" He always said it so seriously followed by a deep laugh.

The funeral director looked at me inquisitively. Why would such a simple question cause a bit of laughter in such a serious conversation? It was a frustrated laugh because I knew I would never hear Curt's antics about his ethnicity again. I looked at my parents and they forced a smile, knowing why I had laughed. I said to him, "It depended on what day it was, but mostly Spanish and Italian." He continued with the questions.

After the form was completed, I had a question of my own. I asked, "Where is Curt right now. Is he still at the Coroner's office?"

What he said took my breath away. "No Amy, Curtis' body is here at the Funeral Home. His body arrived here this morning." Let me just say as a side note that every time someone said 'his body' I cringed. It was the one thing that just pissed me off. To me, he was not just a body. He was my husband, the father of my children, the man I was going to spend the rest of my life with. I felt it was such an insensitive way of describing him.

I could not believe what this man had just told me about Curt. He was here? I was in the same building as Curt was right then? My heart skipped a beat just knowing he was near me.

Once again I asked, wondering what kind of a response I would get, "Can I see him?"

The same answer, "No, Amy. I cannot let you see him."

Damn all you people! Why won't anyone let me near my husband? I felt as lost as I did the day he arrived back in Reno. "Can I stand in the same room he is in?" I asked.

"I am sorry Amy, I cannot let you do that."

"Well then where is he right now?"

"He is down this back hallway and to the right. I cannot even let you stand outside the door to the room he is in, though, Amy."

"Why? Why won't anyone let me be near him? I don't understand! I'm his wife! Somebody needs to let me be near him! I'll at least be able to be near him when he is in the casket at the church, right? It'll just be a closed casket?"

"No, Amy, we are not going to allow the casket to be taken to the church. We need to ask that we have a burial within the next day. Due to the condition of his body, we need to expedite his burial."

The condition of his body . . . words that would haunt and heal me at the same time. It was at this exact moment in time that I learned one of the hardest and most important lessons of my entire life. Even though Curt's "body" was still here, his spirit had moved on. I had to let go of the physical part of Curt and hold onto the spiritual. I had to walk away from this attachment that I had to him physically and search instead for his soul. In our lifetimes, so much emphasis is placed on our appearance and our social status. We are conditioned to believe that what we display on the outside makes up who we are as people. What Curt and I felt for each other was so much deeper than this, though. When all of these people (strangers) were telling me that his body was beyond their help, I had one thing to hold onto—and that was his spirit. I needed to grasp onto the essence of who he was, his soul that had moved from this world to the next. But for now, I needed to stay focused on what I needed to do to honor him on that day.

The funeral director informed us that our next step was to pick out an appropriate casket, a memory book to be signed at the service and cards to pass out to the people attending. Walking through the funeral home on this August morning was a surreal experience. I remember looking at my parents and wanting to say, "What in the hell are we doing here? Let's leave! Curt is coming home! We haven't *seen* him yet!! He may not even be gone! Let's go home and see if he is there!" Instead, I solemnly walked from casket to casket saying things like, "That one does not look like him at all" or "This one is nice but it doesn't feel like it is the right one."

I walked past one that was steel black in color. It caught my attention because it seemed so strong and bold and classic. I internally fell into a momentary depression feeling thankful to find the right casket for Curt. I knew it would be the one that I was going to choose, yet at the same time, knowing it was one of the worst decisions I would have to make in my entire life. We talked for a moment about its features and told the funeral director this would be the one.

After ordering the guest book and the booklets for the service, we sat down one last time with the director. He explained the process of the funeral service and asked specifically, because of the need to expedite this process, that only family members be present at this service. He explained what the procession for the funeral would look like, what he would be saying, and then asked who would be the pall bearers. When we were finished, he shook all of our hands and escorted us out to the front doors.

Walking out of the funeral home that day, I felt exhausted, frustrated, and confused. My world had been turned upside down and inside out. Here I was, again, walking away from a building that held my husband. And again, I was denied the opportunity to even stand outside the door to the room he was in. I had to trust that what everyone was telling me was real and not just a horrifying nightmare. I chose how he would be buried and was told to return the next day with the clothes he was to be buried in. As a wife, how do you respond to all of this information when four days before your husband was standing in front of you, full of life and laughter?

*   *   *

I needed to focus on one thing for the evening. Not only did I need to pick out the clothes to bring to the funeral director for Curt to wear in the casket, I also had to prepare anything that I wanted to put inside of the casket before it was buried. I didn't even know where to begin. That evening I stood in my closet with my sisters and chose what I felt was the shirt, pants, and shoes he was most handsome in. Once again, I felt weak, and sick, and it hurt to breathe. As I looked through each shirt, there was a memory that went with it. This shirt was the one he wore to Easter Sunday, that one was the one he wore when Luke was born.

My sisters left me there to have a moment to myself. Glancing up at Curt's hats, I locked my eyes on the blue and white hat I saw the night the police came to my house. And here I was, looking at it again, knowing he was never coming home, just as I had thought. I began to cry knowing somewhere in my soul I must have known something was wrong that night. I sank down to my knees and rested my head on the carpet. I felt helpless, alone, and scared. My heart literally hurt. As I lay in the fetal position, not knowing how I was going to get up, I heard the sounds of footprints on my carpet. I barely held my head up to see my dad kneeling down next to me.

I said to him, "Dad, I don't think I can do this. I don't know what to do? I just want him to come home. I don't want to live this life without him, Dad." I sobbed into his shoulder.

"Amy, I know you need him. Mckenna and Luke need him. I don't understand why this is happening to you. I want to say to him, 'Curt, where are you? What happened?' But we will never know, honey. I don't know what the answer is."

I wiped my face and looked at the laundry baskets sitting next to us. I pulled out the shirt and swim shorts Curt was wearing the day we left Meeks Bay. They were still dirty from camping less than a week before. I held them up to my dad and said, "He was just wearing these a few days ago. This is what he was wearing to your anniversary night. He looked so handsome and happy and alive! And now what? Now we are going to bury him tomorrow? Why? I don't think I can do this, Dad! I don't think I can do this!"

My dad held me that night in the closet as I poured every ounce of tears that I had on his shoulder. He could do nothing for me but console me. My dad is my protector, my hero. He has four daughters that he has loved and taken care of for the past forty years of his life. Now, his little girl was weeping in his arms and he could do nothing to protect her from the agony she was experiencing. If he could have taken it all away from me, he would have. After about a half an hour, he helped me to my feet and prepared me to face my next task.

I made my way downstairs and sat down at the dining room table to write Curt a letter. I couldn't tell you what it said. I don't remember. No one else would be reading it, so I am pretty sure I spilled my heart and soul to him . . . as if he were sitting right in front of me. If I had to guess, I would say that I told him that Mckenna, Luke, and I would forever be in loss of his unconditional love. I probably told him that I would do the absolute best that I could to raise them the way he would also have wanted them to be raised. I am sure I promised him that they would learn about the incredible father and person he was and that we would all keep him alive in our hearts each day.

I finished the letter, kissed it, put it in an envelope, and sealed it. I also chose a few more items and pictures to place with Curt—like a picture of our wedding day and a picture of the day each of the kids was born. The most significant items I chose, though, were Mckenna and Luke's blankies. They had others, but these were the ones Curt covered them with each night, and now I was asking the funeral director to do the same for him. It was a piece of Mckenna and Luke that gave them great comfort and security, and I knew Curt would be honored to have them. I gathered all of the items and gave them to my Mom. I wasn't going to have the energy to wake up the next morning and take the clothes, blankies, letter and pictures to the funeral home, so my parents agreed to take them for me.

Walking my parents outside, I glanced up at the night sky and couldn't help but wonder where in these Heavens my husband was. A bright, bold, shining star caught my attention. It was much more superior to the other stars and I thought to myself, "That star is Curt's star. Every time I look in the night sky and see this star,

I will think of Curt." I sat for a moment and stared at its beauty. It was unlike any star in the sky that night. What I did not know is that Brian was in the backyard at that exact same time with Mckenna. He was pointing to the same star and told her, "Do you see that star, honey? That is your Daddy's star! Every time you see that star, I want you to think of your Daddy. You can tell yourself that it is your 'Daddy Star'".

We all walked into the house, myself from the front yard and Brian and Mckenna from the back, under the same sky, wishing on the same star . . . with the same loss in our hearts. Within a half an hour, Mckenna and Luke would be asleep, lying on their Daddy's pillow, underneath the star-filled skies that held him.

CHAPTER FOURTEEN

Honoring Him

MONDAY, AUGUST 4, 2008

The morning of the funeral service was filled with agony. None of us could wrap our minds around the fact that we were about to lay Curt to rest. It was decided that the kids would not be present. It would only be the adults attending this service. There was no possible way that I felt I could explain to my two and four year old children that their father was lying in the casket that we were about to see. There may be varying opinions about this, and I think it would need to be a personal choice, but it was something that I was not mentally prepared to deal with. I was worried that they would be terrified and always remember the moments spent at the cemetery instead of remembering their last moments with Curt.

Misty and her husband Gary joined Chet, Aaron, my family, and I on the ride toward the Mortuary. A few of my sisters and their husbands rode with me in Curt's truck. It made me feel like he was with me by riding in his truck. When we arrived, there was a Hurst parked in the front, which I noticed immediately. My first concern was when they were going to bring the casket out. It would be the first time that I would have been within feet of him, so I kept my eye on the door. Curt's family was gathered in the parking lot.

The Funeral Director approached the truck where I was sitting in the front in between Jon and Brian. He asked if I was ready to go up to the cemetery, in which I said I was. He then said, "Would you like to ride in the front seat of the Hurst to escort Curt's body to the burial site?"

I asked, "When will the casket be brought out to the car?"

He replied, "It is already there, Amy. We are ready to begin as soon as you are. Would you like to ride with him?"

I felt a wave of nausea throughout my entire body. I absolutely froze! I was not prepared for this. I had waited all of these days to get within feet of Curt, and he was lying in the car right next to me the entire time?? I was terrified, so it was my instant reaction to say, "No, I am ok right here, we will follow behind him in his truck." My heart was shouting at me, "He is right there????? Lord God, help me please!! I need to be near him! I need strength!! This is not happening right now! Please give me strength!" In his truck, though, is where I stayed as the procession of cars began their drive towards Curt's final resting place.

Watching the back door open and my brothers, my dad, Chet, and Aaron carry Curt's casket toward the plot he was to be buried in, his little brother escorting behind, was the most surreal experience of my life. I stood and watched in mournful disbelief. This was as close to him as I had been since leaving him in the garage just five days before. Now here we all were gathered to lay him to rest. Once he was placed above his plot, there were several words spoken, including my gratitude to everyone for their love, devotion, and support of Curt. A few more family members spoke and then we all stood in a moment of silence.

The most astonishing thing happened during this moment. On what was a calm, sunny day, we unexpectedly were taken over by a huge gust of wind, which surrounded the entire area around Curt's funeral service. The trees were blowing as the wind swirled all around our families gathered there to honor him. I remember it was so powerful that I almost couldn't breathe. And then, within an *instant* . . . it was gone. As quickly as this wind surrounded us, it disappeared—leaving a quiet calm. We all looked at each other, feeling the same thing. It was Curt . . . he had been there. He was saying goodbye.

Walking away that day was sickeningly emotional. I did not want to leave him there. Jon was walking next to me, and I turned to look back one last time. There were two men standing next to the plot where Curt had been lowered in. They had shovels in their hands and they started digging the dirt and throwing it into the hole. I could hear the dirt hitting the casket and I was horrified. I wanted to run back and push them out of the way and tell them to stop. Why couldn't they have waited until we left? Jon put his arm around my shoulder and said, "Come on, Amy. You don't need to watch this. We're taking you home." We drove away from Curt, in his truck, looking back every few minutes to make sure he was okay.

I went home that afternoon and looked at Mckenna and Luke. They had no idea that we had just said goodbye to their father. I felt in my heart that it was the best thing I could have done. There is no way they could have grasped that their Daddy was inside that casket, being lowered into the Earth. At the ages of four and two, I know it would have terrified and confused them. It terrified and confused me. The only thing I could do was hold them in my arms and give them as much love as their Daddy and I could give them. Our sweet angels had lost their true love.

Tuesday, August 5, 2008

On this, the morning of the Memorial service, I woke up and prepared myself to face another day of this life without Curt. Jaimie was meeting Carrie and me at our church to discuss the service with our pastor, Scott. On our way there, we picked up the newspaper. Carrie turned to the obituaries and found Curt's picture. There he was in the paper, a summary of his life and his death written beneath his picture by my brother Pete. I took a deep breath and exhaled. This was not real. This was not happening. I closed the paper and then I closed my eyes. It isn't really possible to sum up the worth of a person's life in one newspaper column. What Pete wrote was as close to perfect for Curt as you could get and I am so thankful for that.

Carrie and I joined Jaimie in the church parking lot where we walked in to meet Scott in a conference room. The three of us had been going to this church for over ten years. When I met Curt, he really had no opinion of his faith. He was not raised in the church and was not fond of spending time there, either; but the one person he enjoyed listening to and felt he connected with was Scott. If, on a particular Sunday, Curt knew Scott was preaching, he would go with me every time.

Seeing Scott made me feel so much less panicked. He knew this was going to be one of the hardest days of my life, so he guided me through the process. I had one question burning in my mind which I had to ask. "Scott, the last few weeks, Curt and I have not been to church. We were camping and he was scouting this trip, and then he went hunting. I am so worried about this and I don't know why. Will this affect Curt in any way?"

Scott replied, "Amy, I would be bothered if you *had* been in church the last few weeks. You and Curt were doing exactly

107

what God would have wanted you to do. You were out there in nature, connecting with Him in a totally different way. When Curt was out there hunting, that was his way to get as close to God as possible. That is where you both *should* have been, out in the world. God would not have wanted it any other way."

This was true. Curt would always come home from a hunting trip and explain to me that there was no other feeling like being out there in the middle of the mountains. There was a connection for him to life that he had never felt anywhere else. He said it created this calm and peace in him that he was so thankful to have. I knew Scott was right and was relieved I had asked the question.

Once all of the details were covered, we planned to meet back at the church later that afternoon, about an hour before the Memorial service would begin. It was going to be a day filled with memories and tears. Jaimie, Carrie, and I left the church knowing we would be returning to honor a man whom words could not justifiably describe.

*   *   *

My sisters, parents, and a few close friends sat in a waiting room down a back hallway of the church while my brothers and Misty helped usher people towards their seats. Preparing for an event like this is unexplainable. In writing the words I would speak for Curt, I felt the pressure and the honor of trying to describe Curt to those who may not have known him. Some of the guests attending this memorial service knew Curt far better than others. I wanted everyone to walk away feeling like they knew what a loving father, devoted husband, and incredible friend he was.

When Scott informed us that everyone was seated and that it was time to begin the service, I pulled together every ounce of courage I had to stand up and walk, arm in arm with my dad, towards the sanctuary. My family and I followed Scott through a side door where I saw about 300 of our friends and family members joined to show us their support. I could feel the love and grief permeating from the room. Mckenna and Luke, once again, were not at this service because, not only did I feel it would confuse and scare them, but I also knew what I needed to do—and was not sure I could, had they been there. The only two children who attended were Tanner and Jake. We knew they would be old enough to understand. My sisters, parents, and I were ushered to the front row where we sat and mournfully watched the service unfold.

Scott began in prayer and then spoke so eloquently about Curt and the man he knew him to be. He then introduced Kim and Carrie to speak. Continuing to watch from the front row, my three sisters and their husbands all walked up onto the stage. They were united in supporting first Kim, and then Carrie, to speak about Curt and the brother he was to them all.

Kim began by speaking of many family memories while snowboarding, dirt bike riding, Christmas tree hunting, or camping. She also talked about Curt's love for his younger brother. Curt and I raised him from the time he was ten years old until he was thirteen. Curt loved and cherished his relationship with his brother, allowing us to provide him with stability in a tumultuous time in his life. It was one of the greatest honors of Curt's life. He was so proud of his brother and loved him with every ounce of his heart.

Kim reminded us of all the things we would miss about Curt, including his handsome smile, his "What's up bro?", his nicknames for everyone, and his love for life. Carrie then spoke of our last night spent together, as a family, for my parents' 40th wedding anniversary just days before he left for his trip and the last moments I spent with Curt in our garage. In her final words, she said, "Amy and Curt and their family were in the best place they've ever been. If there is any peace to be found in Amy's heart during this time, it is that she knows how much Curt loved her, really truly loved her. And now . . . . Amy has something that she would like to share."

This was it . . . it was time for me to honor Curt through my words for him. I began to stand up and had a hard time finding my legs underneath me. I could feel Curt saying to me, "Come on, baby, I'm right here! You can do this! If anyone can do this, it is you! I'm right here!" While my sisters descended from the stage, my dad helped me stand and escorted me up the stairs. We joined my brothers, who remained there to support me. As I began my speech, I knew that four of the greatest men I would ever know stood behind me as my strength: My dad, Pete, Jon, and Brian. I felt, as I began to speak, that they were the force that held me up and the courage behind my voice. As a young woman standing on a stage to speak in front of friends and family, I learned how incredibly powerful the support from these men was to me. These are the words I spoke to Curt:

On the day Curt and I got married, I wanted to write him a toast, but I didn't find the time, and I have always regretted that. So my toast now is to his life and his legacy. I wrote it for him and felt I needed you all to hear it. It's a bit long. I had a lot to tell him, so sorry—if you could bear with me.

> Curtis, my love and my life,
> It's me honey, it's your wife.

We vowed to be forever.
Are you really here?
My forever isn't over yet,
I need you to be near.

People say you can hear me,
Some say you're even here.
I pray to God it's true.
I need to make a few things clear.

I don't know if people know
About the man you really were.
I feel I need to tell them,
I need everyone to be sure.

Do they know how much you loved me?
That the love was real and true?
That you didn't always know how to show it?
That you didn't always know what to do?

Do they know how you told me *every* day
Just how much you loved me?
That our life was good and happy and full,
It was as perfect as life could be.

Do they know that your life hasn't always been kind?
That there's a soul and a spirit that you've had to find?
But it was there all along,
It was just buried deep.
You found your way through us all,
Now it's in our memory to keep.

Do they know that you were strong?
You were solid and true and real?
You taught us how to get up and live,
You taught us how life should feel.

Do they know about your babies?
That you loved them with all of your might?
They were your passion for living,
They were your hope and your light.

Do they know that your face lit up
The second you'd see them each day?
You didn't watch them grow from the side,
Your hands have molded their way.

Do they know you brought Mckenna flowers
As often as you could?
You believed in the smile that lit up her face
As every father should.

Do they know that during Luke's swim lessons
You had to be the one
To get in the pool with him every time
For the bond of a father and son?

And what do you know right now Curtis?
What do you see where you are?
Are you close enough that you're with me?
But really so very far?

Do you know my parents don't know what to do?
You were as close as a son could be.
You know they want to fix it right now.
They can't fix it this time for me.

Do you know that Jon was right by my side
When they came to tell me the news?
And when it was time to bring you home,
Jon and Brian were by your side, too.

Do you know that Brian brought her a flower?
It was beautiful and pink.
We put it in the vase with the flower
That you brought to her just last week.

Do you know that Pete took care of it all?
I wanted you home on that day.
And he wrote the hardest part of it all for me.
He knew exactly what to say.

And do you know that Misty, Aaron, and Chet
Were here before I knew what to do?
They've helped with things you don't even know
And it was all in their love for you.

I don't know what to say about my sisters.
I've tried to write it again and again.
I can't express on this paper what I need to say.
So many stories and remember whens.

So this day will all end,

People will all go away.

What do we want them to know?

What do we want to say?

That life is too short

To think it all through.

This is the lesson

I've learned from you.

So I will try to slow it down.

I'll try to take it in.

In this here today, gone tomorrow

World we're living in.

I won't blink.

I love you baby.

I cried as my dad held my hand down the stage that afternoon. I knew as a family we had said everything we needed to for our guests to get a glimpse of the man that Curt was. We sat down together to watch the slide show that had been prepared with much love and care by Jaimie's husband Chad, our close friends Rick and Kendra, and Misty's husband Gary. It was, to me, one of the most important pieces of the service and I will always be eternally grateful for their help in preparing it. The pictures were accompanied by pieces of the songs, "Hero" by Enrique Eglesias (our wedding song), "Daughters" by John Mayer, "Remember When" by Alan Jackson, and "Don't Blink" by Kenny Chesney. When the slide show was over, and Scott had given his final prayer, we adjourned for the reception held at a nearby historical park, where Mckenna and Luke joined us to celebrate their Daddy's life. (A special thank you to my friends and fellow teachers at Double Diamond Elementary and Hidden Valley Elementary for hosting this beautiful reception and showing my family such an incredible amount of daily support. Love to you all).

I believe that in a day like this, a person only has one chance to convey their emotion, love, and admiration for the loved one they have lost. Curt lived an entire life of happiness, sorrow, strength, pain, devotion, love, determination, and honor. He battled past family demons and found hope and light in his life where others might have given up. He was a lover and a fighter and a protector of all things important to him. When the world punched him down and told him he was not good enough, he fought his way back up and proved the world wrong. He turned his life into everything he knew it was worthy of being and that is why I loved him! It is a difficult task to honor a person's entire life in one afternoon. My family and I did the best that we knew how in the small amount of time we were given, and yet—it would not have been the same if you had not had the chance to meet him yourself. Curtis was, and will always be, unforgettable. We miss you, my love.

PART THREE

Hope

CHAPTER FIFTEEN

The First Few Weeks

The last part to this book, entitled Hope, is about the healing our family has found in dealing with this overwhelming loss in our lives. As I write this, it has been close to three years since the day we learned of Curt's death. So many emotions and events have transpired to bring us to the place we are in right now. It has been a journey that has tested our faith and broken our spirit. Our family has had to choose each day to join together and find strength and meaning to this life where not a lot of meaning could be found.

As I was working through my grief on a daily basis (many times on a minute-to-minute basis) I searched for ways to help me heal. I found in several books I read that there is something called "The Five Stages of Grief". I am going to say, for me, I wanted to throw each book I had that included these stages out my window. I never once tried to "fit" in a certain stage. It wasn't like I would be having a difficult day and say to myself, "I must be in the 'denial' stage." Or I would be having a better day and say something like, "I'm so relieved to be in the 'acceptance' stage." I am sure that anyone who grieves feels a lot of the same emotions. I firmly believe, though, that each person's day looks vastly different from another's who may be reeling with the same type of loss.

I chose instead to honor what I was feeling *when* I was feeling it. If I was walking through my kitchen on a Saturday morning and it brought back a memory of Curt making breakfast for the kids and this made me sad, I'd cry. I didn't cry quietly to protect anyone or only cry a little bit. I would sit down and outright cry until I felt the wave of grief pass. If I remembered something funny that Curt did on a particular day, I would laugh (sometimes out loud), which is what would make me feel better. I rolled with each punch that was thrown my way and dealt with it the best way I knew how at that given moment.

Most of my days were filled with agony and sorrow. I honestly felt at all times like a phantom wandering from room to room in my house, searching for my lost love. Anything that I tried to comfort myself with just brought me more sorrow. I was still living in the life that Curt and I built . . . trying to fathom how to make it through each day without him.

The only ounce of sanity that I carried with me was knowing that my children needed me to get out of bed each morning and provide stability in their little lives. There was not a single day that I spent in bed with my covers over my head trying to pretend this was not our fate. Mckenna and Luke were not able to do that, so neither would I. Instead, along with the immeasurable support from our family and friends, we began to walk in the journey that would become our new life without the man we loved. In all actuality, I felt like a boxer in a ring in the middle of the fight of my life. I had been absolutely knocked out, not even sure how I was going to get up. But when I did, you had better believe that I came back swinging.

In looking for strength one morning while the kids were still asleep, I began to sift through a large envelope filled with cards from friends and family that were brought to Curt's memorial service. Reading those words of support and love was one of the things that brought me comfort and hope in the days and months following his death. While looking through each card, I came across an envelope that said, "For Curtis Conner's family". I opened it and could *not* believe what I held in my hands. The entire staff from the local Starbucks closest to our home had signed a card to Luke, Mckenna, and I offering their condolences. Every single person on the staff, about twenty in all, wrote a tiny paragraph with words such as, "Curt was the sunshine of our morning. He was always so animated and loving life," or "Curt was our favorite customer. He always brought a smile to our faces," or "Our mornings will not be the same without seeing his smiling face. Every time he came to our store, he managed to make us laugh and smile." One message said, "Curtis made everyday special at Starbucks. He always brought laughter to our hearts. We always enjoyed joking around and talking about our kids together. He loved his family *so much*."

I sat in complete and utter awe as I read these messages. I knew each day before Curt went to work, he would go to Starbucks to get a cup of coffee. I didn't know he went in and made friends with the entire staff. One employee even wrote, "For the five minutes Curt was in the drive-thru, he constantly made us smile and laugh. He had been a regular as long as the store and I have been around. It'll be hard not seeing a familiar face." What an incredible feeling to know that he affected others in such an impactful and positive way. The employees at Starbucks did not have to take the time out of their day to sign a card for him, but I am thankful (especially for Mckenna and Luke) that they did.

When you live in a small community like I do, it is astonishing and humbling to receive the level of support that I have been honored enough to feel. I could write an *entire* book about my friends and how they wrapped their arms around me and helped me learn how to live again. Each card had the most beautiful words of condolences, each bouquet of flowers was sent with love, and each phone call was filled with the most heartfelt of words. Every ounce of contact or bit of encouragement I received was taken with gratitude and appreciation.

I know, for example, when Jaimie stayed the night with us two or three times a week, or her husband Chad (one of mine and Curt's best friends, as well) came over every day to check on the kids and I or even to bring my garbage can in for me, I could feel the blessing of love being brought to us. When Curt's friend Russ, who also works in the concrete business, personally made Curt's headstone for us and guided me on how to design it, I could feel the blessing of support being brought to us.

Shortly after Curt's death I received a call from my friend, Brandi. She was coming over to bring a package to me. I remember I was standing outside in the front yard with my sisters when she and her sister-in-law, Michelle, (also a good friend of mine) pulled up to the house. They stepped out of the car and handed me the most amazing gift from the community that I could have asked for. It was a basket filled with love from all of their friends to try and help me in the weeks and months to come. It had gift cards to about twenty places in town, including the car wash, movie theaters, restaurants, and more. It had games, coloring books, crayons, markers, puzzles, stuffed animals, a music CD and more for the kids. I also found candles, books, cozy socks, fluffy blankets, and other comforts inside for us.

While I was so touched by the generosity of the contents of the basket, I knew this is not what I was most thankful for. It was the care that went into creating the basket. All of these people pulled together to try and find a way to comfort us in an inconceivable time of need, just as all of my friends had done. They were trying to pass on hope to a family that they knew was walking in the valley of the shadow of death. Although they knew they could not take us out of the valley, they provided some beauty for us to see, some hope for us to find. Like all of the prayers, cards, gifts, flowers, prepared meals, or phone calls I received . . . I was, and still am, eternally grateful for all of my friends. I could tell story after story and still not do justice to honoring all of the people who rallied around us.

After Brandi and Michelle left my house that day, I drove for the first time to the cemetery by myself. I had not been back since the day we buried Curt and was feeling like I needed to be near him. As I pulled into the cemetery and alongside Curt's grave, I felt such overpowering sadness. It took me five minutes to even get out of my car. I sat with my head against the steering wheel, tears pouring down my face. I remember feeling my heart race and my entire body shake. Braving my emotions, I opened my car door and stepped out onto the paved road.

Walking around my car, I could see the freshly placed grass over the site that he was buried in and beautiful flowers covering the entire area. With each step that I walked closer to him, I began to cry more and more. I tried to remain calm so that I wouldn't end up in hysterics, which was a difficult thing to do. Sitting down next to his grave, I took a deep breath trying to take in the scene that surrounded me. Slowly my words started pouring out to the man I loved. I tried to tell him everything I was feeling, which at one point turned into words of anger and fury. There I was, sitting in the middle of a cemetery, shouting out loud towards my husband's resting place every single reason why I felt pissed off and enraged for the loss of his life. I was not, and never have been, mad at Curt *or* God for this fate we all have suffered because I knew it was an accident. I just felt anger for the tragedy that had become our life. I felt angry that Curt would never see Mckenna and Luke grow up and that they would have to experience their lives without him. I felt an anger inside of me knowing Curt and I had built this life together and our family would never be able to live it the way it was intended to be lived.

My words slowly began to turn into a sorrowful bawl. I finally had no more words and could only begin to sob. My weeping was gradually matched with a low wail, which honestly scared me. The flood of emotions I was feeling was being released and I could not have stopped it even if I wanted to. I could hear myself crying which terrified me because I didn't know where it was coming from. I could only think in my mind, "If anyone hears me right now, they are going to think I am being tortured or hurt by someone." However, I was the only one in the cemetery that afternoon, left to unleash this anger inside of me.

After about twenty minutes, I fell silent in exhaustion. I had emptied my soul and could release no more. Quietly crying now, I crawled over to the fresh grass directly above Curt's grave. On that warm August afternoon, I lay my weary body down above where his lay and struggled to gather the strength I would need to return to the life we now lived without him.

That night I wrote in my journal:

August 10, 2008

> *Curtis, my love, I went to the cemetery today. It was the first time that I have been there since we buried you. I need you to know that I am sorry for the moments I was angry. It is a part of what I feel—but not with you. With life. For handing us*

what we have been handed. I didn't know I was
capable of feeling or releasing such pain inside of
me.

I feel so incredibly awful and strange and sad
that the kids have not been within even ten miles of
you since July 30th when you kissed them goodbye.
I don't feel ready to take them to the cemetary
because I can't even tell them you are there. They
believe you are in Heaven, so how will they possibly
understand that you are there, too?

When Lukey and I were lying in bed, tonight, I
said, "Daddy loves you Lukey." He said, "Daddy no
come home to us," and I said, "No, he wants to but
he can't." He said, "Because he died?" Oh, break
my heart. Seriously. Yes, Luke, because he died.
And the saddest part is that this two year old tiny
love doesn't even know what that means. Honestly.

Like tonight, he was looking for his blankie
and he could not find it. He looked all over and
said, "Mommy, my blankie died". What does that
mean now—if he can't find it or if it disappears, it
dies? Oh, my heart.

Mckenna starts her first day of Kindergarten
tomorrow, as you know. I am going to believe with
all of my heart and soul that you are going to walk
in with her, let her sit on your lap, and comfort her
on her first day of school. OK, honey?

I need strength and comfort in falling asleep at
night. I told Misty the other day that I want to buy
a twin bed because our bed feels so big and lonely.
I am also very scared that I am going to fall asleep

and something is going to happen. The other night I was going to sleep and thought I was not going to wake up. Like what if I fell into such a deep sleep that I wouldn't wake up. In fact, I woke up several times and felt the kids' backs to make sure they were still breathing.

If it had been light out, I wouldn't have panicked. But the nighttime is so unsettling to me. In my sleep last night I heard the pounding of someone knocking on our door so clearly—just like that night. But it was an illusion, a dream. A nightmare really. This is all just a nightmare really. I love you Curtis. I miss you and I love you and I am scared without you.

Love Your Wife

CHAPTER SIXTEEN

Bundles of Joy

The next morning, I woke up and knew what my main goal was. It was to get dressed and ready to go, with a smile on my face, to take Mckenna to her first day of Kindergarten. My sisters and I had decided that all of our kids needed to maintain as much normalcy in their schedules and days as possible. The plan all along had been for her to start. Being four years old, she would be the youngest one in her class, which meant that I could have waited for another year for her to begin. There was so much madness going on around the house, though, that I knew it would be good for her to have her own space and time away from it all. She would also be in the same class as her cousin, Ty, which would comfort her.

After getting ready, I came downstairs and greeted Mckenna. I could either make or break this first day for her. If I showed her I was sad and heartbroken that it was really her Daddy that was supposed to be taking her to school, she would become scared and upset. So even though my heart was shattering into a million pieces, I put on my bravest face and prepared to leave.

We decided to take her in Curt's truck. Kim, Carrie, and I were the ones who took her and Ty. Sitting behind his steering wheel was a very difficult thing to do. He spent so much time in this truck, and now it became my role to drive it. I didn't want this role. I didn't want to move the seat up and readjust the mirror so I could see. I didn't want to undo a single thing that he had done, but that was not my choice now.

When we got to school, I waited for Mckenna's teacher, Alyssa, to open the door. Being a good friend of mine, she was obviously well aware of our situation and ready to guide Mckenna through her first day of school. It had only been eleven days since Curt's death. A week before we were burying Curt, and now his little girl stood to face her first day of school. I thank God for Alyssa's presence on this unbearable day. She was the guardian angel for us in such a confusing time. I knew that Mckenna was safe with her and Alyssa would watch and take care of her. Not many teachers have to deal with a child starting her first day of school under these circumstances. Alyssa was everything to Mckenna (and for me) that we could have asked for.

Handing Mckenna off to begin her first day, however, was the challenge. She was glued to my leg, upset and crying. I know in any instance this would break a mother's heart. Multiply that heartbreak by one thousand and you would have an idea of how I felt. Finally prying her off of my leg, Alyssa looked at me, straight into my eyes, with a calming confidence and said, "It's OK, Amy. I've got her. I've got her. Everything will be OK. I'm just going to take her in and she will be fine." And within five minutes, Mckenna had calmed down and *was* fine. *I* had calmed down and was fine. She did it, my brave, little girl. With much love from her teacher and supportive prayers from her family, she did it! Later that day I wrote:

August 11, 2008

Hey babe, were you with her today? Mckenna grew up so much, and it is unbearable that you were physically not here to see her. She went to her first day of Kindergarten <u>and</u> she got her ears pierced!! She was terrified to do both—but took it on and tackled it and afterwards was so proud of herself! It broke my heart to take her to Kindergarten without you. Alyssa even let her ride the little pony down to the office to take the attendance down. Kim, Carrie, and I all watched from the window in my classroom. I was so proud of her—and I know you were, too! I just believed with all of my heart that you were in there with her reassuring her that she was ok. Kim and I picked her up at the end of the day and she was <u>great</u>!! She even made a best little friend! What a big girl we have!

I told her last night that as a privilege she could get her ears pierced because she had asked if she could. Can you believe that? She wanted her ears pierced like Anna's. So Kim, Jake, Jaimie, Anna, Carrie, Luke and I took her. She was scared at first but she did it! And within an hour she was fine!! I wish you were here to see it all! I long for you honey! I ache for you! I don't want to do all of this and experience all of these firsts in our life without you! I am scared and lonely and my heart aches for you. Are you with me? I need you and I miss you.

Love Your Wife

*   *   *

After I dropped Mckenna off at school the next morning, I took Luke to Carrie and Brian's house and found my way to their computer. For the past few days, one of the only things that had been running through my mind was the conversation Curt and I had by his truck the day he left. His words rang perfectly clear in my mind. "Every kid needs a dog while they are growing up. Ours are no different." He was going to look for one for the kids when he got home. If Curt were here, this would have happened—so I was going to make it happen for him. I got online and began to research Puggle puppies, which are the mix of Beagle and Pug I had discussed with him that day. I found a site that breeds them and would ship them from Oklahoma to their new families.

I began to click on picture after picture of available puppies, looking for one the kids would love. I wanted to get a girl for Mckenna, but hoped Luke wouldn't feel sad because he didn't have a boy pup. I really didn't want it to become an argument for either of them. I considered that at night they both would want the puppy to sleep on their bed. Therefore, with much thought (okay, clearly not a *whole* lot of thought) I chose to order a little boy puppy *and* a little girl. Yes, that is right, I ordered *not* one puppy . . . but two!! What was I thinking? I knew everyone was going to think I was crazy on this one. The brother and sister pups would be arriving by airplane, in the same little crate, within three days.

I stood up from the desk, took a deep breath, and walked downstairs into Carrie's kitchen where she was standing with my mom and Jon. I was relieved Jon was there because, like all my brother-in-laws, I knew he'd have my back on this decision. Jon and I have this unspoken signal where we can read each other's reaction to things and we signal that we know what the other one is thinking. We call this signal "22", because we would point two fingers towards our own eyes and then to the other's eyes—as if to say, "I see you; I am watching and I know what you are thinking right now". The two eyes to two eyes is our "22". For example, if we were with a group of people and something was said that reminded me of Curt, Jon would give me the "22" to say, "I heard it. Don't worry; I'm right there with you. You can do this."

On this particular morning though, the signal meant a bit more than it normally did. Upon announcing that I had ordered something for the kids that would warrant me to claim temporary insanity, Jon looked at me and said, "Oh come on Amy, what could you possibly have ordered?"

I calmly replied, "A puppy." At first, I only told of one pup just to see what kind of reaction I would get. When my mom turned (I think to ask Carrie if I had lost my mind), I looked at Jon and held up two fingers.

He quickly gave me our "22" signal and quietly mouthed, "I know!! You're in so much trouble!" He laughed out loud!

My mom looked back at us, not knowing we were having this little banter, and said, "Amy, you don't even know the first thing about a puppy! I trust you, but why would you do that?"

I replied, "I don't know Mom, I felt in my heart that Curt really wanted the kids to have a dog growing up, so I wanted to do that for him."

She looked at Carrie to continue their conversation. I quickly looked at Jon and whispered, "NO! *Not* "22", I am saying I got TWO dogs!!" Jon looked like he was going to fall off of his barstool!

When my mom turned back towards us, Jon said, "I think that is a great idea Amy! Curt did want the kids to have a dog and I think it will be a good distraction for them right now."

Out of the corner of my eye, I could see Jon was looking at me like, "Have you lost your ever-loving mind?? *Two* puppies?? What are *you* going to do with *two* puppies?"

I knew I had to tell them all the truth. I tried to talk Jon into making the announcement for me, but he wasn't going for it. I looked at Carrie and my mom and hesitantly said, "*Actually,* I didn't really order one puppy . . . I ordered two. There will be a little girl puppy for Mckenna and a little boy for Luke. They will be arriving by airplane in about three days. I really just need you all to help me and not be worried about this. I know it is crazy and will be a lot of work, but I think it will bring some joy to Mckenna and Luke in all of this sadness."

My mom, being one of the *most* caring, devoted, and loving people I know, did not even hesitate in her support for me. She was the sanity behind many of my decisions during this time and I counted on her to help keep me grounded. However, nothing about this decision was sane, and she knew it. Everyone in my family had basically been helping me function in my life for the past few weeks. Taking on the responsibility of two puppies would not only affect me, but it would also affect them. Not to mention, my family had never even had dogs while we were growing up; so, I had no idea what I was getting myself into and my mom knew it. With very little hesitation, though, she supported me because she knew how much it would've meant to Curt. Ordering these puppies for me was not just bringing joy to my children; it was providing Curt a means of being involved in their lives through his wishes.

That night, I had the first of only two dreams I've had of Curt, in which I felt like he actually visited me, since he died. In the dream, I was walking through the airport to pick up the puppies. When I looked ahead of me in the terminal, I could clearly see Curt sitting on the ground with his back against the wall. He was playing with our two puppies that I was on my way to pick up. In this dream, he never once looked up at me. It was as if he didn't even know I was there. He was laughing and playing with the puppies while they jumped all over him. It was so real that I felt like I could reach out and touch him. I felt like this was his way of telling me he was happy with my decision to get these two little puppies for our children.

When in a dream state during sleep, our minds are relaxed and open to any connection with our loved one who has passed from this life to the next. It's a way for them to visit you without scaring you, in a time when you are in a subconscious state. Curt never actually came to me or communicated directly with me after he died. I know there are people who have seen or feel they can speak to their loved one. It has never happened for me in that way, nor has it happened for either of our children. This was one of only two times in a dream where I felt like Curt was trying to tell me something, in which I woke up feeling like he was really there.

If you have never experienced the loss of an immediate family member or friend, you may not understand at all what I am explaining. If you have, you know that in any hope of getting a sign or message from them, your mind remains open to any plausible possibilities. This dream was a gift to me, and I am thankful to have received Curt's blessing on the puppies we would soon have in his honor.

August 15, 2008

>*Curtis the puppies are here. We named the boy Hunter and his sister Roses. Most fitting, don't you think? Jon came up with the names. Hunter is because you loved to hunt and Roses for the name you used to call Mckenna. They came from Oklahoma together in the same crate. Kind of like my favorite book, "Where the Red Fern Grows". Do you remember three weeks ago when I told you that you really needed to read that book? I wish you were here to see them. Where are you babe? Are you sitting next to me right now? I am completely and utterly lost without you! Why us?? What was the purpose of this accident? Why? I love you Curtis. I've got it covered—I don't know how, but I've got it covered babe —*
>
>>*I love you and miss you-*
>
>>>>*Love your wife*

On a side note, I would like to say that Mckenna and Luke fell instantly and madly in love with these puppies. This was one of the best things I could have done for them in their healing process. I don't really suggest this as a means of therapy, considering that my family is really the ones who cleaned up after them and helped me take care of them. These puppies were such hard work, like having another baby in the home—except twins! But the kids, including all of their cousins and any child visiting our home, were very much distracted from our personal chaos with the love they felt for these two little bundles of joy.

Chapter Seventeen

Necessary Pain

August 17, 2008

Well, honey—it has been over two weeks since you left to go hunting and I am still certain that they have the wrong person and you are coming home to me. Nightime is completely unbearable to me. Someone is staying the night with us every night. Last night it was Julie, tonight is Carrie. Luke, Mckenna, and Jake are having a sleepover on the office floor.

I watched a home movie with the kids today. I stare at the pictures constantly and cannot remember your talk and your laugh—because I try too hard. It made my heart so happy and sad at the same time to see your face and hear your voice. You blew a kiss to the camera and it instantly took me back to the afternoon in the garage when you blew me a kiss. Luke looked at the t.v. and got <u>so</u> excited and said, "There's my daddy, mama!" Little ray of sunshine.

Everyone was here again tonight. Pete has worn his camo shorts over every single night for the last two weeks. He just loves us so much. Dad wore his camo shorts over the other day (on his Harley) with black motorcycle boots and a blue t-shirt. Love him!

I miss you so much it hurts, and am scared to be without you. Really scared. Please guide me through this darkness. I love you.

Love Your Wife

As the days wore on, so did our grieving process. Where one day we would find strength and hope in something, the next day it would bring us sorrow and pain. One of the bridges we had to cross was closing down our business, American Concrete. A few weeks after Curt's death, my dad and I spoke of the need to complete the jobs that were still running and attend to the bills that needed to be paid. Being very much involved with the business, I knew exactly how to take care of the paperwork side of most things, such as the billing, invoicing, taxes, and payroll. My dad made it clear to me that as each day proceeded, so did all of the payments we needed to make on the trucks, equipment, and other liabilities. With only a few jobs left to finish, meaning our income was quickly going to come to a stop, I needed to make some decisions about the future of the company.

My choices were to sell the business, which I couldn't do knowing it was Curt's dream that I'd be handing to someone else, become business partners with someone who was willing to run the company with me, or dissolve it. The thought of seeing our logo on trucks around town and the business still running without

Curt made me sick to think of. I knew there was only one thing to do and that was to dissolve what Curt and I had created. We still had jobs running, and thank God for Gary and our foreman, Matt, we were able to complete the work and receive payment on the jobs. Once the work was complete, I had the difficult task of terminating employment on all ten of our employees, most of whom had faithfully worked for Curt for years.

My dad was my rock through this chaotic time because there were days that I didn't want to pull myself off of the ground due to grief, and he was making phone calls and meeting people at Curt's shop for me to keep the company afloat. Daily, I would meet my dad, sometimes hours after he would arrive, at the shop to begin the difficult task of properly closing down the business. In time, we sold all of the equipment (including small tools, generators, a bobcat, several trucks, and an entire warehouse of concrete items). While my dad was meeting people for these sales, I was in the office canceling all of our insurance policies, business licenses, payroll accounts, credit accounts, and filing monthly and quarterly taxes. I really wanted to be at home comforting my babies, but time wasn't on my side in closing everything down. Payments would need to be made where there was no income to support it.

I remember receiving a phone call from my friend, Pat, who owns a local business where American Concrete supplied a lot of its materials from. We had just finished a very large job and still owed his company, Tetrus, a substantial sum of money. Pat was calling to tell me that not only did he wipe our balance clean, but he also needed a copy of the liabilities I owed to the other businesses in town. He was going to call each business to explain to them what he had done and ask that they do the same. As a local business owner, and a friend, he felt the need to help me, knowing what I had laying ahead. I was a young widow with two young children and an entire business I was needing to close in an unsteady economy. I was completely humbled by his effort in helping me, knowing this would take time (*along* with the money he cleared for me) away from his business.

I may be wrong, and Pat can correct me if I am, but most local businesses responded to Pat's request and helped me in one way or another. Any of the national businesses or national concrete companies he called said there was nothing they could do for me. What an amazing lesson to learn as a business owner and consumer. The local businesses took care of their local people in need. The larger out-of-state companies really had no connection or desire to help someone they didn't even know; therefore, they chose not to. In any purchases I make today, I try to support our local businesses. Curt always explained to me that we needed to support our community and purchase our supplies through them. This is why he worked with Pat at Tetrus, and now I understood even more clearly why. Thank you, Pat!

August 20, 2008

> *Hi babe—hard day yesterday and today. Really hard. I've had to make a lot of calls to vendors—and some people didn't even know you were gone. One man called your cell phone the other day. I answered and he said, "I know this is a strange question, but is Curtis ok?" I told him that you are not ok, that you passed away. He said he heard something was going on and he didn't believe it. He was trying to get a hold of you.*

I know you were and are loved by the community, but it is overwhelming really the grief that everyone is feeling over your loss. I mean, people that truly have cried and grieved over your loss. I called Les Schwab today to pay a bill for the business. The manager was so incredibly upset. He said that when he heard the news, he cried for us. He said he loved you and your friendship and honestly grieves for your loss. He also said that the first time he met you, the two of you struck up a conversation—and an hour had passed before he even knew it. You were so interesting to talk to. Do you know how many people have told me that? That they talked to you and before they knew it an hour had passed and you had completely engaged them. Amazing!

Mckenna asked me in the garage the other day if I was going to give away all of your stuff. I am not sure why she even asked that. You know, she has hardly talked about anything. So this question knocked me over. I totally assured her that I am wearing your ring, and all of your clothes are staying in the closet—and everything is staying exactly as it is. The only thing changing is that you can see us, but we cannot see you. Painful.

The other day in the kitchen, Luke heard Brian, Carrie, and I talking about the boat. He said, "I ride in the big boat with my Daddy?" Brian got up and walked away crying. I said, "No babe, Daddy can't come with us on the boat this time. He is in Heaven. But he can watch you go in the boat."

He said (which he says often right now) "I want to
go to Heaven with Daddy!"

I have to explain to him that this is not our time
yet. So he said over and over, "I go in the big boat
and Daddy watch me!" My heart is just breaking
into a million pieces, and once I pick the pieces all
up, something else happens and it shatters all over
again.

*   *   *

As the days wore on, so did my journal entries—which brings us back to the morning of August 21, 2008, when Kim called me with the news that Ty was certain Curt had visited him. In the early morning hours, Curt came to Ty to give him the message that no one needed to stay with me anymore because he was always with me, keeping me safe and everyone could go home. What an enormous message to receive from such a young, little boy.

What was most astonishing was that Ty (along with all of the kids in our family) was not told that I had people staying with me each night. During those three weeks that had passed since learning of Curt's death, I had people in and out of my house all throughout the days. With the nights being the hardest time for me, though, at least a few members of my family continued to stay at my house with me. We worked together through this incredibly chaotic and confusing time while they helped me care for mine and Curt's two children, Mckenna and Luke.

Ty, however, slept at his own house, in his own bed, and was not aware that I had this help. At the age of five, he definitely did not understand the concept that I may have felt scared being alone at night. For him to tell me that everyone needed to go home because Curt was keeping me safe was not something he could have made up. My dad was the one who was supposed to be staying at my house with us that night, which is why I called to tell him I would be ok without him because I knew Curt would keep me safe. I knew this would be the first of many messages I would receive from Curt.

On August 23rd, my family decided it was time to drive to Humboldt County and find the exact place where Curt lost his life. It was time to find some sort of closure in knowing exactly where he was when he passed away. We felt the need to make a wooden cross to place near the location that he died. First thing in the morning, we started our journey to Humboldt County. My dad, Pete and Julie, Jon and Kim, Brian and Carrie, and I split into two separate vehicles (one being Curt's truck) while my mom stayed with all of the kids. It was such a somber morning because we all knew that, for the first time, we would see where Curt took his last breaths.

About an hour into the drive, while sitting in the backseat of Curt's truck, I quietly called the Coroner's office in Reno with a question. There was something that still did not make sense to me. I kept going over and over it in my mind. When I was given Curt's wedding ring and Leatherman the day he arrived in Reno, there was an inventory sheet attached to it. It had listed the following items: Wedding ring, Leatherman in case, bag. I could not figure out what the bag was. The coroner only gave me the first two items. Why didn't they give me the bag? It made no sense to me. I felt that I needed to get that bag, whatever it was.

I finally got a hold of a woman working with the Coroner's office. I explained the situation to her and told her that I really needed someone to find out where this bag was. She assured me that she would look into what happened to it and why it was not given to me. She would call me back as soon as she knew anything. She remembered the investigation and would be sure to give me any answers she could find.

I hung up feeling like I had accomplished something. The past few weeks had been such a whirlwind and I wasn't sure what day it was, let alone what had been taken care of. I had to get that bag back so that I could see what was in it. I glanced around to everyone around me. The car was pretty quiet and dismal. Everyone was trying their best to keep it as light as possible, but we all knew we were making the same exact drive Curt had made just weeks before. We were passing the same buildings, signs, and scenery. The only difference is that he had no idea it would be the last time he'd make this drive.

After about ten minutes, my cell phone rang. The caller ID showed the number to the Coroner's office. My heart skipped a beat. I hoped that she had some answers for me. I could instantly tell by her tone, though, that there was a problem. "Amy, I don't know quite how to say this. There was a mistake that was made. When the Coroner's office in Humboldt County sent Curt's personal items with him, they listed all of the items that came in the van. The bag that they listed was actually the bag that they brought his body to us *in*. I am so sorry honey. I've never seen the actual bag listed as an item. I'm sorry, Amy."

I hung up the phone and looked out the window, tears streaming down my face. One blow after another. I couldn't even speak. Why would they list the bag, and why was this not explained to me? I braced myself for the flood of emotions this news would bring to me. Even though I didn't want to, I imagined, for the first time, Curt being placed in a bag. Do you know how terrifying this is for a wife to have to fathom? I quickly had to push this image out of my mind, knowing it would be bring me an entire new wave of grief.

We arrived in Humboldt County just a few hours later. Using Curt's GPS unit to guide us, we began to make our trek back into the mountain range. His hunting partner who was with him the night he died had also given Jon and Brian very specific directions on how to find their camping spot. As we continued our drive down this narrow and rocky road, it was perfectly evident why Curt was not able to bring our camping trailer with him. This was not a road that had been frequently traveled on, causing our cars many times to slow to a crawl. We found ourselves often with only inches of road between us and a drop off next to us on the right side of the road.

Once we made it to the area where Curt would be hunting, we began to look for his camping spot. His friend informed us that Curt had taken his truck in the tall dry weed that surrounded their spot and driven in it several times in a large circle to push the weed down. We would know exactly what we were looking for when we saw this track that Curt had created. The moment we spotted it, my heart sank. It made everything so real. Their camping spot was located right next to a beautiful river, which was surrounded by trees. It sat in the foot of the mountains and felt peaceful and serene.

Standing in this tranquil location, we began to look for one very specific thing. It was explained to us that every time Curt walked in front of the entrance to his tent while he was setting it up, he stepped into a gopher hole. It quickly became the joke between Curt and his friend, causing Curt to say, "By the end of this damn trip, I am going to fill this hole with every single beer can we drink." Little did he know that this is how his family would find the location of where his tent once sat.

Once the Humboldt County police left Curt's friend to pack up their camp, he took the few beer cans they had emptied the night before and buried them in the hole in front of where Curt's tent lay. Pulling out a shovel, Jon walked around to different holes in their campground and began to dig into the fresh dirt, listening for the sound of these cans. Finally, after about ten attempts, Jon threw his shovel into a hole and hit the pile we were listening for. We all froze and looked at each other, then watched him pull up a mound of dirt mixed with several beer cans. It took us a full minute of silence before anyone spoke.

Knowing the exact setting of Curt's death brought me an overwhelming wave of emotion and relief. From the night I learned of his death, I could only imagine where he was when he took his last breaths. I didn't have to wonder or imagine anymore. I was looking at the exact place he climbed into his tent and said goodbye to this world. This was it. I knew now that he passed away in the middle of nature, with the sound of water rushing next to him under what was probably a pitch black, star-filled sky.

After many moments of silence, Pete grabbed the two boards we would need to make the cross, a nail and hammer, and a carving knife. Once he hammered the cross together, I sat down and began to carve Curt's name. Little by little, the letters formed on the board to say CURTIS. We painted the letters black and hammered the cross into the ground under the trees that billowed next to the river.

On our drive home that night, I couldn't help but think of all of the things we had been through to that point. It brought me back to a time when our lives had been so calm, predictable and safe. Within a flash, that security was taken away from us, forcing us to learn how to survive. Glancing up at the night sky, Curt's star caught my eye. For Mckenna, this star had become a sense of comfort. Each night, it became her custom to walk outside and say goodnight to Curt while looking at this star. This evening, I was doing the same thing from Humboldt County, knowing that a chapter in this nightmare had finally been closed.

*   *   *

A few weeks after our trip to Humboldt County, a package was delivered to me through UPS. I didn't recognize the return address. Sitting alone out in my driveway, I opened the box wondering what could possibly be inside. What I saw made me literally want to faint. I felt light headed, causing me to drop down onto a knee. Inside the box was Curt's lantern, the same lantern that emitted the carbon monoxide, causing his death. There was a note inside from the Humboldt County Police Department stating that they had sent it in to a lab as part of the investigation to determine whether or not it was defective. If it had been, then the company may have been liable for his death. It had been their conclusion that the lantern was not faulty. They were sending the lantern to me now so that I could also have it tested for possible defects.

Through the delivery process, the glass to the lantern had shattered. There were shards of glass spilled throughout the entire box. I was in shock that this lantern would have even been sent to me without my knowledge it was coming. I closed the box, stood back up, and walked it over to my garbage can. I didn't even hesitate in my decision to just throw it away. I didn't want it anywhere near me. It would consume my already depleted energy, which I could not afford to do. Instead, as in with all my days, I walked away knowing my focus needed to be on healing my family, not on something like the lantern that I would never be able to change. You have to pick your battles in life, and this was not going to be one of them.

I faced plenty of challenges and pulled from any strength I had to deal with them. The most significant included: receiving the autopsy report (and then the death certificate) by mail, celebrating Mckenna's fifth birthday only five weeks after Curt's death, visiting the cemetery for Curt's birthday and watching the kids sweep off his headstone to place their flowers on it, and going back to work (which I quit every single day for the first week. Thank God my principal stuck with me and would not allow me to quit.)

I remember facing people for the first time in public, at events or grocery shopping. One of the first things people would do was glance at my hand to see if my wedding ring was on. I also remember filling out a form for the first time and having to mark the box next to 'widow' instead of 'married'. Through these events, I became stronger and stronger until I had no choice but to get out of bed and face the world head on. I just needed to realize that God would be the one to provide my strength, all I needed to do was just ask.

CHAPTER EIGHTEEN

Pockets of Hope

This chapter represents all of the healing I found during this time. I was in search for little pockets of hope wherever I could find them. These pockets would be where I stored my strength for each day. Obviously a huge one for me was my children, who gave me the courage to get out of bed each day and live. My family was right there with my kids, giving me the support I needed to put one foot in front of the other. My faith pulled me through, knowing that Curt was now in Heaven where God was taking care of him. Finally, my friends gave me the confidence and encouragement to live each day to the fullest, knowing they would be by my side to help me through.

Beyond the healing I found from these core lifelines, I relied on two other sources of comfort to heal me: music and the messages I received from Curt. Music guided me through some of the most difficult moments in this process. There is something about music that touches my soul in a way that is hard to describe. I can hear a song and it pulls emotions out of me that I didn't know existed. Much of the music I listened to was country, but not all. Some people say country music can be sad and depressing. I have to disagree wholeheartedly. For me, some of the best, most real stories have been told through country songs.

There is a song sung by Brad Paisley and Dolly Parton called, "When I Get Where I'm Going". It makes me think of one of the things Curt would tell me if he could. A few of the lyrics say this:

> When I get where I'm going
> There'll be only happy tears
> I will shed the sins and struggles,
> I have carried all these years
> And I'll leave my heart wide open
> I will love and have no fear.
> Yeah when I get where I'm going,
> Don't cry for me down here.

Another country song that reminds me of Curt is also sung by Brad Paisley. It is called, "Waiting on a Woman". In the song, from the moment this man meets the woman, he is waiting on her. He waited on her for their first date, and to get married to her, and anytime they went anywhere—but to him, she was worth the wait. In the last part of the song, he says:

> I've read somewhere statistics show
> The man's always the first to go
> And that makes sense 'cause I know she won't be ready.
> So when it finally comes my time
> And I get to the other side
> I'll find myself a bench, if they've got any.
> I hope she takes her time, 'cause I don't mind
> Waitin' on a woman
>
> Honey take your time, 'cause I don't mind
> Waitin' on a woman . . . .

148

Not all music was country. Many songs pulled emotions out of me, which help me heal—such as "No One" by Alicia Keys. Her lyrics say:

> I just want you close
> Where you can stay forever
> You can be sure
> That it will only get better
> You and me together
> Through the days and nights
> I don't worry 'cause
>
> Everything's gonna be alright
> People keep talking
> But they can say what they like
> But all I know is
> Everything's gonna be alright
>
> And no one, no one, no one
> Can get in the way of what I'm feeling
> No one, no one, no one
> Can get in the way of what I feel for you, you, you
> Can get in the way of what I feel for you.
>
> When the rain is pouring down
> And my heart is hurting
> You will always be around
> This I know for certain.
>
> You and me together
> Through the days and nights

I don't worry 'cause
Everything's gonna be alright

I remember there came a point in time when I couldn't cry anymore. I literally had run out of tears. My soul was empty and I could not cry, but I felt like I needed to. I feared bottling my tears and not being able to release them. Luke even walked up to me one morning and said, "Mommy, you don't miss Daddy anymore? You aren't crying today". Poor Luke, he really had no way of gauging my emotions. Being two, he only recognized angry, happy or sad. Because I hadn't been crying, he thought I didn't miss Curt anymore.

The fact was, though, that I missed Curt to the point that I didn't know *how* to cry anymore. I eventually found that the only thing that would pull this emotion out of me was music. One day, Carrie and Brian found me in my office, sitting at my desk, with a slide show of pictures of Curt flashing across my computer screen. I had a playlist of songs that reminded me of Curt blasting on the stereo throughout the entire upstairs. Luke and Mckenna were with Julie, so I knew they wouldn't have to worry about the state I was in.

I sat in the chair at my desk and bawled. Tears streamed down my face while I listened to the words of these songs. Carrie and Brian came upstairs, wanting to know why I was purposely doing this to myself!! Didn't I want to turn the music off and stop? I told them I needed to do this! I desperately needed to find a way to release the pressure and pain I felt in my heart, and this was the only way I knew how. It seems like this may have hurt me more than anything. It honestly was the only thing I could find that would help.

There is one song I listened to that day that I most want to share with you. It is "No Air" sung by Jordin Sparks and Chris Brown. I have marked which lines are sung by Chris and which are sung by Jordin. This song hit me harder than any other, because she asks how she's supposed to breathe with no air. I found the irony to be that Curt died from the loss of his. This is what the lyrics say:

Jordin

If I should die before I wake
It's cause you took my breath away
Losing you is like living in a world with no air

Chris

I'm here alone, didn't wanna leave
My heart won't move, it's incomplete
Wish there was a way that I could make you understand

Jordin

But how do you expect me
To live alone with just me
'Cause my world revolves around you
It's just so hard for me to breathe

Chorus

Tell me how I'm supposed to breathe with no air
Can't live, can't breathe with no air
That's how I feel whenever you ain't there
There's no air, no air
Got me out here in the water so deep
Tell me how you gonna be without me

If you ain't here I just can't breathe
There's no air, no air

Chris
I walked, I ran, I jumped, I flew
Right off the ground, to flow through you
There's no gravity to hold me down for real

Jordin
But somehow I'm still alive inside
You took my breath, but I survived
I don't know how, but I don't even care

So how do you expect me
To live alone with just me
Cause my world revolves around you
It's so hard for me to breathe

*   *   *

There was one other factor that was key in my healing process. It was the communication I received from Curt through a channel I was not expecting. This is the part of the story where I asked that you keep an open heart and an open mind. Anyone experiencing a significant loss knows that one of their main concerns is that their loved one made it safely to the other side. Any sign that is offered can cause an intense amount of comfort and relief.

There have only been a few people who have been able to offer me these signs from the other side. If their information had not been so specific, I am not sure I'd believe the way that I do. One of these people was such an unexpected source that I didn't know how to react in the moment. It began with a phone call to woman who I had seen regularly in the past few years for massages. She also worked in energy healing, which I had dabbled a bit with. Learning about my Chakra levels and how they affected my daily living absolutely fascinated me. On this particular morning, though, I called Terry to ask that she help me. This was the first time I had contacted her since Curt's death.

Terry and I really only knew each other on a professional level. While she knew that Curt had passed away, she really didn't know many details. I was calling to tell her that my energy levels were completely depleted, and I needed her to help me find some strength again. She invited me over and we spoke of what she could do to help me. She asked if I wanted her to do an energy healing, body work (a massage), or have a reading. I didn't really know what a reading meant, which I told her. She said she thought it would be a good idea if we proceeded with a reading and see where we needed to go from there.

Reluctantly agreeing, I sat in a chair across from hers while she closed her eyes and began to focus. She asked that I close my eyes, as well. After much silence, sitting across from each other, she said to me, "Amy, Curt is here. He is standing right behind you."

In my mind, I thought, "Ooooohhhhhhhhh, a *reading*. I get it *now*! She's going to do a *reading*!!" I opened up one eye and peered around me to the left, and then to the right and didn't' see anything. I thought to myself, "OK, Terry—if you think you see Curt, then give me what you got, because it's going to have to be pretty specific for me to believe".

She proceeded to say, "First of all, Curt is saying that he woke up after dying in such a fog. He didn't know where he was or how he got there. He knows you are in shock and not knowing how to

153

deal with his loss, but so is he. He cries and is homesick because he only knows being there, in your home with you. You are both grieving your losses on each side." This made me so sad to hear. I wasn't sure I believed yet what she was telling me, but if this was true, I felt so sad.

She then asked, "In your house at night, you may hear noises. Is this true?"

Still not really convinced, I said, "Yes, this is true. I think I am just sensitive to them because I am scared and alone."

She said, "He wants you to know not to be scared, because it is him. He is trying to tell you he is there. He also visits Mckenna and Luke in their dreams. This is the only way he knows how to speak to them without scaring them."

Knowing all of this was probably very valid information, I still was in need of something more specific to allow me to feel like Curt was really there. Terry continued.

"He is telling me something about jewelry. Did something significant happen with jewelry in the past day or so?" I explained that our friends Dianne and Marissa had bought Mckenna some earrings that were extremely special because they were Curt's birthstone.

Terry said, "He is happy someone gave her something to remind her of him. His birthstone is Topaz, right?"

I agreed that it was, but tried to think of every way she could have known that. She could have seen his obituary in the paper and figured that out. I was reaching for anything to convince myself that this could not be real. Come on, Terry . . . give me something I could hang on to.

"Curtis would also like you to know that he knows about the star." *What????* Shivers ran through my entire body. How did *she* know about the star??? She continued, "It brings him comfort to know that you talk to him through the star, and so does Mckenna."

That was it! She really had to say no more. There is no possible way she knew that a star would have so much significance to me. That was the thing I was looking for to tell me that Curt was there with me. I began to cry, giant tears running down my face. She said, "Anything you can do with the kids to remind them of their Daddy makes him feel like he is still in their everyday life. He thanks you."

We sat in silence for a moment while she tried to see if there was anything else he wanted to tell her. I'm pretty sure she didn't mean to switch gears all together, but she suddenly said, "I just saw puppies running across my vision. Is there something about puppies? Did he have puppies when he was little, or do you want puppies?" I began to laugh out loud through my tears! I could not believe she said this! Our two little pups, Hunter and Rose, were what she was referring to. I explained that I just bought the kids two puppies about a week prior.

She said, "Curt is very happy about these puppies. They will give Mckenna and Luke a place to put their love that he is not able to give them". The only word I could use to describe the way I felt at this moment was 'stunned'. These were very specific things that brought me such instant healing. I felt like I didn't even know how I ended up in this chair across from this woman whom Curt was speaking to me through. After closing the session with the message that Curt loved Mckenna, Luke, and I and was taking care of us in any way he could from his side, Terry opened her eyes and looked at me. I couldn't even speak for about two minutes.

I wiped my tears away and finally said, "Terry, you saw him. I can't believe you saw him. That is unbelievable. Thank you so much! I know now that he is ok. I feel such completeness knowing this. Thank you, Terry!" I left her house that day honestly feeling like I had been hit by a train. My head was spinning and I felt the most relief I had felt since learning of Curt's death. I wondered when my next message would come from him.

It came sooner than I thought it would. Just weeks later, my friend, Dr. Annette Childs, invited me to a session with a group of people who were going to meet with a nationally recognized medium. A medium is said to be someone who is able to bridge the physical world and the spiritual world to engage in communication with spirits. Annette, being someone I trust with all of my heart, and the other influential person in my healing, asked if I wanted to be a part of this session. Having an open mind, knowing Curt had already contacted me once, I wanted to see if this medium could tell me something specific, as well. Having read Annette's books, <u>Halfway Across the River</u> and <u>Will You Dance?</u> opened my mind to new possibilities. About a week later, I found myself sitting amongst about twenty of the most amazing people I will ever meet. They had also lost a loved one and were trying to find a connection with them.

When it came time to direct her focus to me, the medium said, "Amy, Curt wanted me to tell you that he knows in life the two of you were admired together, but because of your love for him, people *continue* to this day to admire your strength as a couple. He also wanted me to tell you that he knows about the earring you lost."

In complete shock, I lowered my head and began to cry. I knew exactly what she was talking about. Weeks before, the kids and I had moved into a new house. It was not going to be possible for us to stay in the house we shared with Curt. We had to walk away from that home, and all its memories, to find the house that we now live in today. Before we moved, however, I realized that

I had lost one of the diamond earrings Curt had given me for an anniversary present one year. I was beside myself trying to find the missing earring, sick to my stomach that I may have lost such a special present from Curt. Sadly, by the time we moved into our new house, I still had not found the earring. With about twenty of my close friends and family in and out of the house helping me move, I knew I'd never see it again and I was distraught.

Her message continued, "Curt wants you to know that the earring is not important, Amy. It's a material thing and you need to let go of it. He is not mad that you lost it. He wants you to know that you can let it go because it is not important."

On my way home that evening, I resolved in my mind to listen to the words he sent me and let go of the earring. What was most important was that he loved me enough to give me such a beautiful gift. The earrings were just a way of showing me his love, but they were not something I needed to be upset with myself for losing.

Two days after my meeting with that medium, I was in my bathroom getting ready for my day. I reached down into the drawer that held all of my hair clips. There, sitting on the back of a flower barrette (perfectly placed) was the diamond earring I had lost!! When I called my sisters to tell them I had found it, Kim explained that it was practically impossible that I had. She said that during the moving process, she had taken all of my bathroom drawers and dumped them into one big box. Upon arriving at the new house, she pulled the contents of the box and quickly divided them among the drawers in my new bathroom. How that little earring could have landed delicately placed on this little flower petal was beyond her. I never second guessed it for one minute. I knew how it made it safely back to me, and that was all that mattered.

Chapter Nineteen

Help Them Heal

Children need to be guided in their grief. Losing someone special to a death is a confusing, sorrowful, and frightening experience. Adults have a hard time dealing with and working through their emotions when a loved one has died. Can you imagine how many confused emotions children are trying to manage? I witnessed this first hand with Mckenna and Luke. It is a dreadfully agonizing experience to watch your children suffer in such a way, knowing that you cannot help them. The only thing a parent can do is love their children and support them in their healing. It is a helpless feeling because you want to protect them and make it all better, but sometimes in life this is just not possible.

I have several friends who had lost a parent when they were young. One story was imprinted in my mind, though, and made a huge impact on the manner in which I have helped Mckenna and Luke heal. One of my high school friends spoke to me of the loss of her mother when she was Mckenna's age. She was never really told of her mother's death, as if nothing ever happened. In the days, months, and years that followed, the memory of her mother slowly faded. All of the pictures of her came down and the stories of her eventually disappeared. My friend grew up longing for the mother she would never know, holding onto any piece of information she could find about her.

If there was one thing that was inscribed in my mind about this story, it was the tremendous ache my friend felt in her heart to know more about the parent she had lost. She searched for anyone who was willing to offer a story to her about her mother's life. She realized that her father's pain in losing her mother was greater than the need to keep her memory alive. I agree that it is such an agonizing feeling to be in constant pain for the loss of a spouse, and may be easier for some to just push the memory of them out of their mind—but not at the expense of a child's need to remember them. Everyone grieves in different ways, and no one is better than another in this. I passionately feel, though, that it is not our right to take the memory of a parent away from a child, when they so desperately need to know them.

In the weeks and months following Curt's death, everyone in my family wrote down everything they could remember about Curt. They would write funny stories and fond memories. Some wrote about his mannerisms and others wrote about his annoying little habits. Mckenna and Luke will be able to look back at this, along with pictures and home movies, and hopefully have a collective remembrance of the most influential man who will ever touch their lives. I pray this book ties a lot of those memories together for them.

A child's grief, however, is much more than remembering the loved one they lost. It is about the daily walk they will take for the rest of their lives without them. This is not something a child should ever have to figure out for themselves. There is a plethora of emotions that accompany grief, which is doubtful that a child can work through on their own. I learned this the hard way with Mckenna. About a year after Curt died, Mckenna began to withdraw in a way I hadn't seen before with her. As a parent, I did not know how to help her through this. It appeared in her day to day life, with school and her friends, that she was happy. On the outside, she looked like a bubbly, resilient five year old little girl. On the inside, she was falling apart and needing to talk about her emotions in losing her Daddy. I realized that she was now at an age where she may need to receive grief counseling.

As I began to search for a counselor, I realized a startling need in our community for grief therapy services for children. I called several offices and found that children's grief therapy was not as easily available as I had thought it would be. There is an organization specifically designed by a friend of mine to offer group therapy, which we tried, but Mckenna was in need of speaking to someone individually about her Daddy and her methods of dealing with his loss. A group setting seemed to be a bit overwhelming for her. After much research, I decided to try my luck with a family therapist. It was by the grace of God that this counselor was able to make a connection with Mckenna through play therapy. She slowly helped to pull some of Mckenna's emotions out of her heart, which allowed her to begin to open up about her pain.

It was not until Mckenna began her work with this counselor that I began to see true healing in her heart. Even though she looked like she was coping with her father's death, she was slowly slipping deeper and deeper into her grief for him. My sisters, their husbands, my parents, my friends, and I were always right there, ready to listen to her and talk her through anything. What I didn't realize was that she needed someone outside of her personal support network to talk to. In part, I think she didn't want to upset anyone, especially me, by crying and releasing her emotions. She knew we would tell her anything she wanted to know about Curt, and spoke constantly about him, telling stories of his love for her. She was in desperate need, though, to grieve her loss with someone new.

I feel so blessed to have found her counselor, Natalie. I know that if Mckenna had not felt a connection with her, this would not have worked. Mckenna fell in love with her almost instantaneously. They formed a bond, which allowed Natalie to help her begin to heal. She continues, to this day, to teach her skills in working through her grief and has brought back a light to Mckenna's eyes that had faded in time. From the first day she began counseling, she began to open up to me bit by bit.

In remembering a conversation we had the night after her first visit, Mckenna said to me, "Mommy, did you know that I have dreams about Daddy. I'll dream that he is real, like he is alive again. But when I wake up in the morning, I realize it wasn't real at all. It makes me so sad". It was the first time she actually spoke to me about losing her Dad. I knew right then that this therapy would be exactly what Mckenna was going to need.

A few months ago, I started to see a shift in Luke, as well. Being two when Curt died, he really had no concept of what was going on around him. Now, at the age of five, he was becoming aware of his loss in a completely new way. He was old enough to understand now that his Dad was not coming home. One day he said to me, "Mommy, what if I go to Heaven and I cannot find Daddy?"

I said, "It's OK, Lukey. You don't need to find Daddy, he will find you!"

"But what if he doesn't recognize me?" he said.

"Honey, why would he not recognize you? Of course he will recognize you!"

"But what if I die when I am old? Daddy only knew me when I was little. He won't recognize me if I am old when I die."

What a deep thought for such a little boy to have. I replied, "Maybe when we get to Heaven, we all look like we did when we left each other. Please don't worry, Luke. He will find all of us, and we will all be together again."

He emphatically stated, "Well, when I see him, I am going to be running and screaming for him." I am sure that he will be, too.

Luke loving his blankie and his Daddy at a soccer game

Little conversations like this pop up all of the time. Mckenna has been the most vocal during the last year. She once asked, "Mommy, did you put anything in that box with Daddy when you said goodbye to him?"

I realized that she thought I had the chance to say goodbye to Curt and she didn't. I replied, "Mckenna, I never got to say goodbye to your Daddy. I was never able to see him to say goodbye to him. The last time I saw him was the same day you did. Did you think all this time that I was able to see him but you weren't?"

"Well, yes. I didn't really know," she said.

"Oh, honey. Do you want to know how I said goodbye to him?" I walked her into my bedroom where I pulled out my journal to him. I showed her a few of the entries I had made, in which I spoke to Curt as if he were sitting right next to me. I explained that when I had prayed to Curt, I felt like I didn't know where to direct it to, but when I wrote to him, I knew he could see my words. I pulled a brand new journal out of my nightstand drawer and gave it to her. I said, "Mckenna, why don't you keep this journal for your Daddy. You can write to him like I do. Just tell him everything you want him to know about your day and how you feel about him. He will see it, honey."

She took the journal with enthusiasm straight to her room and closed the door. I wondered what she would write. I told her that she didn't have to share it with anyone, not even me. So, I didn't know if she would keep her words to herself or not. When I began my journal, she was only four years old. Now, at the age of seven, she possessed the skills possible to reach out to her Dad in the same way. I was proud of her for taking the opportunity to try.

About a half an hour later, Mckenna opened her bedroom door and walked into my room carrying her new journal. She held it out to me and said, "Mommy, I wrote to Daddy. Do you want to read what I said to him?"

When I opened her journal, I found three pages full of the most beautiful writing I had ever seen from her. She had written about a dream she had of Curt that she wanted him to know about.

She wrote to him that in her dream we were on a walk with the puppies in the field behind our house, when all of a sudden Curt appeared. He held her hand while they walked, and after a while, she said to him, "Daddy, do you want to come home with us?"

When he replied yes, we began to walk back to our house—except this was to our new house, not the one we lived in when Curt was alive. He asked her, "Where are we going?" She told him that we were going to the new house and she would take him there and show it to him. I honestly was astonished by the depth of her writing. I did not even know she *had* that dream. She wrote to him as if he were sitting right in front of her. It was amazing! Ever since that first entry, she will take the journal places with her and write to Curt about her experiences. It has become a central piece to her healing.

Throughout the past three years, I have lived and learned through a child's grief. Just as with anyone's grieving process, it is so evident that every child grieves differently. My kids felt more comfortable in private counseling than group therapy. Knowing that our community already offers group grief therapy for children, which can be successful, I knew I had to do something to help families also locate and have access to individual counseling services for children who have lost a sibling or parent. My family and I have been working to create **The Hope in Healing Foundation**. With time, we will be able to launch the fundraising for this organization.

A portion of the proceeds from this book will be donated to The Hope in Healing Foundation. We will be working closely with specific counselors who have a background in grief and play therapy. It will benefit children through age eighteen in guiding them through their grief. The foundation will be a means of information, resources and licensed counselors for families who need a place to turn to following the loss of a loved one. It is going to take time, and a lot of work, but I am dedicated to this cause and will make sure, in Curt's honor, that it becomes a source of healing to the children of our community.

CHAPTER TWENTY

Lessons I've Learned

SHOES NOT AVAILABLE

My entire family was gathered at a party one time when a guy close to my age approached my mom. I was busy keeping conversation with a group of friends and did not even know this little "talk" was taking place. I have to admit this gentleman was young and good looking and probably even a bit my type. What he said, though, pissed me off—to be quite honest. He explained to my mom that he was so sorry to hear of our loss. He knew that what I needed was someone to come into my life and take care of me. He said "he could do it" but he was currently in a relationship. It needed to be someone who was good with kids—and anyway, it was a difficult situation because whoever that person was had some "pretty big shoes to fill".

Really?? Who did this guy exactly think that he was? I am honored that someone would take that much time out of their life to think so deeply about my happiness, but I do not need to be "taken care of" by anyone. No one needs to save me. And for the record, Curt's shoes are not available to be filled. Those are Curt's shoes. Why would I want anyone to fill Curt's shoes other than Curt. I would never ask anyone to be him or live up to who he

166

was. That was his job, and he did a damn good job at it! So thank you, dear fellow, for your advice, but you just so happen to have it all wrong.

Oxygen Masks are Necessary

As parents, it is our obligation to our children to be as physically healthy as is possible. If we do not take care of ourselves, it will make it harder for us to take care of our children. I always have felt that I don't have time to eat breakfast because I am too busy getting my kids their breakfast and getting them ready for school. I don't have time to workout because I would feel guilty that I wasn't spending that time with my kids. I shop at the grocery store with my children's meals in mind because their needs come first. While this is all true, their needs are our priorities, there is a major component missing.

As a single parent or not, as a parent dealing with a divorce or a death, or as a married couple, we need to put our health at the tops of our lists. I hear the comparison time and again made to the flight attendant who asks parents to please put on their oxygen masks first and then put on their child's. It is an instinct to want to take care of our children first. It comes as second nature to put our needs before theirs.

I tried that approach in dealing with Curt's death. Everything I did at all times was for Mckenna and Luke. I did not take a second of my time to deal with my own spiritual, mental, or physical health. I felt guilty if they did not have 150% of me because I knew that they did not have their father. I ran myself into the ground. Before long, I had nothing to offer them. I was a shell of a mother continuing to walk down a destructive path. After about six months, my hair began to literally fall out in chunks. I lost about twenty pounds and I knew I had hit bottom in my physical healing and realized something had to change.

This is when I got my gym membership, which was my first gift to myself. I started to carve out time in my day when I might have been doing something less productive. I began by walking for fifteen minutes on the treadmill and increased my workouts as I gained strength. Don't get me wrong, it took me about a year of dedicating myself to my workouts, then stopping, then dedicating myself, then stopping before I got on a regular routine.

It has taken me three years to figure out that eating a solid breakfast, lunch, and dinner is beneficial to everyone, including me. I need to eat healthy meals so that I have the energy to raise my kids the way they deserve to be raised. Eating healthy made me want to spend more time on my workouts. It all goes hand in hand. Not to mention, I have started instilling these habits within Mckenna and Luke so that they can make these choices for themselves when they get old enough.

You might think you are honoring your children by giving all of yourself to them at all times. Honoring yourself first is the best gift you could give them. It will teach them to honor themselves, too.

KEEP MEMORIES ALIVE

One of the greatest challenges as a mother has been to find ways to keep Curt's memory alive. Of course there are stories, pictures, and home movies. But I always think, what is it that would make him proud of us in our effort to show the world that we are not letting his memory go anywhere?

One of the largest contributing factors to our ability to do this is the run that my sisters have organized each year in Curt's honor.

Every September, there is an event that takes place in Reno called the Journal Jog. On our team, "Team Curt", all of our friends and family gather to run or walk in remembrance of Curt (all wearing the same specifically designed shirts). During this event, we are able to show Luke and Mckenna each year how important their father was and still is. The funds raised from the run in the past three years have been donated to their college fund.

This year the focus of the run is going to change. Any proceeds from the event will be donated to The Hope in Healing Foundation. The picture here shows our team the second year we ran, and continues to grow. Every person on the team holds a special place in my heart and I will always be thankful for the time and effort they have shown in keeping Curt's memory alive. Thank you Team Curt!!

PASSING WRONGFUL JUDGEMENT

When I am in my car driving somewhere, I come across people all of the time who are running red lights, speeding through intersections, or not paying attention because there is clearly something on their mind. I notice the same behavior when I am in the grocery store and someone may not be watching where they are going or they have an absent look on their face. In years past, this would easily annoy me. I would think things such as, "Watch where you are going!" or "Slow down!"

Since living day to day life in a personal nightmare, I know what it feels like to be in a grocery store and not even remember making it from one aisle to the next—or standing in front of a row of food with a blank look on my face, staring at something for twenty minutes straight and not even remembering why I was there.

I know what it felt like driving to the cemetery for the first time by myself. Did I make mistakes driving? I am pretty sure I must have. Did I run a red light or was I distracted by the thought of where I was going? Yes, probably so. When Jon and Brian were driving from Humboldt County trying to keep up with the van that was bringing Curt home, did they drive the speed limit and follow all of the rules of the road? I would have to say they were driving in panic and pain—so they most likely made some mistakes, as well.

When we pass judgment on someone who has crossed our path in life, we don't know their whole story. It very well could be that this person is just being careless and needs to pay more attention. It also very much could be that this person just found out their child has been in an accident and is on their way to the hospital. It could be that this person is rushing to their father's side because he is in the last few moments of his life and they need to say goodbye. Their carelessness could be a result of a layoff, an argument, or a cancer diagnosis. We don't know what is going on inside a person's world. I have learned, and try to teach my children, that we need to practice compassion and send a little prayer that person's way. God will take care of the rest. Try not to pass a wrongful judgment and instead pass some love.

Write Your Memories

In watching my sister Carrie raise her son, Tanner, I always admired the way she diligently kept a journal for him. About once a week, she would write down her favorite memories with him or funny things he would say to her. When Mckenna was born, I continued the tradition by starting a journal for her. Every so often I would write stories and entries for her about our life. I pasted in little mementos for her, such as a birthday invitation or a drawing she had made for me. I loved the idea that some day she would be able to go back and read all of the little messages of love from me. When Luke was born, I started his own journal for him, too.

Every few months, I would give the journal to Curt and ask him to write something in it. These little love notes to his kids have become some of the most important things I could give to them. In one journal entry from Curt to Mckenna when she was two years old, he said:

Kenna Bear,

Hi sweetie, your Daddy loves you (the most). Every day when I get home you run up and give me a giant hug. I look forward to this all day.

Love Daddy

In another entry he wrote:

Mckenna,

It's 7:40 p.m. on 3-24-06. You're drinking your bathwater right now which is making your mom ill.

You're a lot of fun Mckenna and we love you a lot.
I gotta go because you want me to take a drink out
of a tea cup right now!

Love Daddy

Mckenna will always be able to look back on these messages from her father and know how much he loved her. Her journal is filled with little notes from him and stories of our life. He once even told her that his favorite thing to do with her was go to 7-Eleven for a slurpee and that she loved the pink flavors with the purple straw. Nobody will ever be able to take that away from her. Writing your memories makes it possible for your loved ones to read about your life for years and years to come. It becomes a part of history that doesn't change form or value. They are your words, so offer them as a gift to your family.

To Luke, Curt wrote:

Lukers,

You are a good boy. We love playing with you
and watching you grow. You love to play with the
stereo buttons and turn around and smile at us. You
seem to really enjoy your sister's antics. You bring a
lot of joy to this family. We love you little man.

Love Dad

His final entry to Luke was just six months before he died. If he had known this, I am sure he would have filled the journal. He wrote:

Luke,

> *I enjoy your playful spirit. You're always ready to play and have fun. You love to throw things especially rocks into the street. You're a good boy. For your birthday I'm gonna get you a Tonka truck and maybe a big wheel bike. You just got a big boy bed (a Car's bed). You always have a smile on your face. We love you Lukey.*

> *Love Daddy*

Family Strength

There are a lot of people who have asked me if Curt's death brought my family closer together. They have seen our strength and unity and the incredible bond we share. What they may not realize is that we were already this close: our Mom and Dad, the four sisters—Julie, Kim, Carrie, and me, our husbands—Pete, Jon, Brian, and Curt, and the cousins—Dylan, Jake, Ty, Tanner, Ashtyn, Mckenna and Luke. This is one of the reasons Curt loved being a part of our family. I am sure if he could, he would thank my family for showing me their unending love and carrying me when I could not carry myself. He sees, just as I have, that our family has suffered this loss together, and every single day we continue to find strength in each other.

When people are tied in the union of family, it can be a difficult journey or it can become one's source of strength. My parents worked hard on our family ties. They raised us to respect and love our family, through good times and bad. I know several people who don't even speak to their family members. Someday, when they lose their loved one, they will realize that life *is* short. They won't be able to get that time back that they missed.

It is my prayer for you today that you are able to reunite a family bond if it has been broken. By the grace of God, the strength of our family has always been this close. It is what has carried us all through. "Grateful" barely describes how I feel about my family, and I pray it's how you feel about yours.

Our only complete family picture at Brian and Carrie's wedding, June 2006.

IT'S OK TO LAUGH

I am just throwing this one in for good measure. Ninety-five percent of the population probably wouldn't make this same mistake. Just in case this helps even one person, it makes me happy to share. One morning, on my way out the door to work, I told the kids to get in the car and get buckled. I wasn't in any particular hurry and we were not running any later than usual (if you know me, you know what this means). After locking up the house and jumping into the driver's seat, I put the keys into the ignition, started the car, and backed out of the garage. Suddenly, there was a thunderous noise, as if the entire house was crashing down around us! It scared me out of my wits!

When I looked in my side mirror to see what in the world was happening, I realized that I had made a major mistake! I turned around to the kids and made sure they were ok and then assured them that everything was fine! I then climbed out of the car, which I had now parked in the driveway, to inspect the damage. Here's what I came to understand.

When Luke got into the car that morning, he had buckled himself into his seat, but forgot to close his door behind him. He thought Mckenna would be coming into the car through his side. When she didn't, he simply didn't realize and forgot to close it. In any *logical* circumstance, I would have walked into the garage, seen that his door was not shut, and closed it for him before getting into the car.

What I do know, though, is that my whole life was nothing close to a normal circumstance at this point. Note to self: this is the perfect time to heighten the heck out of your senses!! Apparently I had plenty on my mind that morning—probably running a list in my head of the errands I had to run after work and what I was going to make for dinner that night, and always thinking of Curt.

It didn't matter. The final product was not looking very pretty. Luke's door had caught on the frame of the garage door and as I reversed the car, it just about ripped the door right off the hinges. It now was bent in half backwards. I tried to shut this mangled mess, but it wouldn't even come close. How many prayers of thanks do you think I was shooting towards Heaven that Luke did not get hurt in this disastrous accident? (I'll just throw one more in there right now: Thank you, Lord God, for sparing my son the pain of my mistake).

Luke looked at me to see what my reaction would be, and you know what? I think I was in such shock, that I just started laughing. It was not a "this is so funny" laugh. It was a "oh my gosh, what did I do???" laugh. Luke said to me (with big blue eyes), "Mommy!!!! Why are you laughing?!! Our door is broken!!! That is not funny!!" What he really meant to say was, "Oh great!! My mom has finally cracked!! She has lost her marbles! Just great!"

I said, "Luke, it *isn't* funny—but you know what? There is *nothing* I can do to fix it. Would it make it any better if I screamed and yelled and got mad?? No—because that also will not fix it!! So the only thing I can do is laugh! What a huge mistake I just made!!"

To the kids, the mistake was that I didn't close the door for Luke. To me, though, it was much more than that. I almost would have felt better if I had been texting or calling someone on the phone. Then there would have been a reason why I wasn't paying attention. I just honestly had a lot on my mind . . . because I have a lot on my plate keeping a house, a family, and a job afloat. After all I have been through, I know that material things don't have a whole lot of importance for me. As long as the kids were not hurt, we could send the car in to get fixed. It would take time and money, but someone would fix it. And to be honest, I didn't really want to teach my kids that yelling and screaming would solve the problem, because it doesn't.

I called my mother, who I am sure was thrilled to hear from me about this. She came to my house to pick us up. We left my beautiful brand new (which doesn't make the story any easier) Toyota Sequoia in the driveway for a tow truck to come and pick up. I couldn't even close the back door at all. It was not the proudest of moments for me. To this day, I am still ok that my only reaction was to laugh. Do you want to know why? Because getting mad could not possibly fix anything; so, I am grateful God was able to grace me with some humor to deal with it.

Chapter Twenty-One

Lessons Learned from Curt

Go Big or Go Home

During the reception which followed the Memorial Service, there was a video camera set up so that our friends and family could record a message for Mckenna and Luke about their father. I look back at that video from time to time and watch the stories being told about the man Curt was. Each message is endearing and unique and I am sure the kids will listen to each word carefully to learn anything they can about their Dad. When I think of the lesson that I learned from Curt entitled 'Go Big or Go Home', I always remember the one that our friend Gary recorded for the kids. It describes Curt's personality so well and is a perfect analogy to what I want Mckenna and Luke to know about Curt.

He says, "Alright kids, I have a little story for you about your father; just a little something to describe his character. We had been playing in a monthly poker group—your father, me, and a group of tight friends. Your father was always infamous for A) being late, (B) bringing Bud Light, and (C) loving Nacho Doritos. So, he'd show up late, buy in, play his hands, lose his money, chips were stacked against him always (it was a short stack at all times) and his famous line was, "Alright, let's bring back the 'all in'. He would shove his chips forward no matter what his hand was, it was always win, lose or draw with him. And nine times out of ten, this is no lie, he would win. At that point he would escalate up and be the strong man on the table. I tell you that because his character was such that he ran his business in a similar way—and his life. When the chips were stacked against him, he would always go all in. He would say to me, in working with him, "You know me, Gary, I'm gonna jump in with both feet . . . and then I'll learn how to swim, or you'll help me figure it out." I was always happy to help him swim.

So in growing up and leading your life and going on in your own adventures, becoming young successful people, I would encourage you to live your life like your father did. In that, I would expect you and would ask you to, please, go out and live life, take chances, and once in a great while, go all in. Your father did, and it worked well for him. I love you both."

What a perfect way to describe Curt. It really was his motto in life to 'Go Big or Go Home'. He never lived it any other way. He lived it to the fullest in each and every moment. I have never seen a person so involved and so enthusiastic about their life as he was. He didn't see the point in half-assing anything, not in his business, or with his family, or in his friendships. Mckenna and Luke need to know this about him, and I hope that they will possess much of this same quality in their lives, too.

Let them Fall

About a week before Curt died, we bought Luke his first bike. It looked, of course, like a little miniature blue motorcycle with training wheels. One evening we decided to take a family walk on the path that ran behind our house. Mckenna rode her bike in front of Luke while we walked behind both of them. At one point, Luke got a little ahead of us and tried to round a corner in the path. His bike tipped over, fell off into a patch of grass, and the bike landed on top of him.

I was instantly by his side, picking his bike up and helping him to his feet. I am pretty sure it scared him more than anything. I wiped the dirt from his shorts and hugged him, asking him if he was ok. Curt walked over to us, picked Luke up and set him back on his bike. Giving him some encouragement, he sent Luke on his way to try again.

Later that night, I was standing in the kitchen when Curt walked in from the garage. He said, "Amy, I have to talk to you".

I had to laugh. "Uh, oh! *That* doesn't sound good."

"Amy, I am being serious. Please listen to me. I don't want you to run to the kids every time they fall and pick them up. Please just let them fall without being right there to help them. I want them to learn how to pick themselves back up sometimes. They will never learn how to be tough if you don't let them. Ok?" He was very serious in his words, and I knew this was a moment that he wanted to express his Daddy concern.

"Ok, Curt. I won't. It was just my instinct to run to him," I replied.

Curt kissed me, "I know honey, I just want them to be strong." So now, as is Curt's wish, I try to just let them fall—and pick *themselves* back up—well, most of the time.

FAMILY TRADITION

If there is one thing Curt tried to create in our family, it was a sense of tradition. I don't know if he was doing this more for the kids or himself. He grew up in a chaotic life as a little boy; so, in changing his destiny, he wanted to be able to look back at our lives and remember all of the tradition we built into our family. In doing so, it has made it possible for us to carry out his wishes after he was gone. Our traditions dedicated to Curt include Father's Day camping trips, Christmas tree hunting (which always begins with breakfast at Bordertown), and dirt bike campouts for his birthday. Looking back in our family photo albums, you can see these events transpire in each and every one. Curt helped to create memories of a lifetime for our family and has guided us in the way we still live today.

Another tradition is Fourth of July. Curt, Jon, my dad, Pete
and a few of the boys.

Life is Short

Curt really had no idea that he was going to teach me this lesson. This was his fate, though, and he could do nothing about it. Life is short. There is a song by Kenny Chesney that I have already mentioned called "Don't Blink". We played it as one of the songs in the slide show at Curt's memorial service. There is a line in it that plays back in my mind every day. It says, "When your hour glass runs out of sand, you can't tip it over and start again. Take every breath God gives you for what it's worth." We don't know *when* our hour glass will run out of sand. It wasn't that Curt's death taught me to live my life in anticipation of someday dying. It taught me to live each day as a gift and be grateful for every minute of it.

I look at it like this . . . . you could live your life as if your hourglass is half empty or half full. It's a choice. I look at my life as half full, grateful for the memories that have filled it to this point. I don't know when or where the sand may run out, but that doesn't matter. What matters is what we have today. Don't lose your today worrying about tomorrow. Life *is* short—so remember to "take every breath God gives you for what it's worth". As I promised Curt in the memorial service, I won't blink.

Be a Friend

There is a country song written by Tracy Lawrence called "Find Out Who Your Friends Are" which describes Curt so well. The lyrics say this:

Run your car off the side of the road

Get stuck in a ditch way out in the middle of nowhere

Or get yourself in a bind lose the shirt off your back

Need a floor, need a couch, need a bus fare

This is where the rubber meets the road

This is where the cream is gonna rise

This is what you really didn't know

This is where the truth don't lie

{Chorus}

You find out who your friends are

Somebody's gonna drop everything

Run out and crank up their car

Hit the gas, get there fast

Never stop to think 'what's in it for me?'

or 'it's way too far'

They just show on up with their big old heart

You find out who your friends are

Everybody wants to slap your back wants to shake

your hand when you're up on top of that mountain

But let one of those rocks give way then you slide

back down look up and see who's around then

This ain't where the road comes to an end

This ain't where the bandwagon stops

This is just one of those times when

A lot of folks jump off

{Chorus}

When the water's high

When the weather's not so fair
When the well runs dry
Who's gonna be there?

Curt was the person who would be there, no questions asked. He was one of the most selfless people I know when it came to helping his friends. If you were to call him at 10:00 at night needing help installing your kitchen cabinets, he would get out of bed and come to help. All of his friends knew they could count on Curt if they ever needed him. I remember one time, my sister Kim came over to our house and she realized that her car tire was almost flat. Without hesitation, Curt was on the ground pulling the tire off and within minutes had replaced it with her spare tire. This is just who Curt was—it was in every ounce of his character. When my friends need me, I want them to think of me the way Curt's friends thought of him. Wouldn't you?

CHAPTER TWENTY-TWO

Final Thoughts

It is my hope in reading this book that you walk away knowing about the man we were so blessed to have in our lives. Most importantly, I hope that you have seen that we choose as a family to celebrate the life he was able to share with us. Through time, we have learned how to live our lives in a "new normal". He is never gone from our memories and our love for him will never become any less than what it is, but the pain has slowly begun to fade. In our walk through this valley, we choose to smile and enjoy life the way Curt would want us to. We have all grown stronger in the past three years, and know that we will continue to do so daily through healing and living.

I have an incredible amount of faith that I will find love again when the time is right. If there is one thing that I will honor for myself, it is that I will not settle for something that may not be right just so that I don't have to be alone. In addition, there is no part of me that wants to find someone to replace Curt. My relationship with Curt is a part of who I am, but not what defines me nor what I have to offer someone in the future. I am a strong, capable and honorable person and am proud of the place I am in today. It is my prayer that the person I find see me for who I am and not for what I have been through.

I am closing this book with twenty-two chapters in honor of my family, who have guided me through each day of my life. As with the signal I share with Jon, I know I can look at every member of my family at any given time and read what they are thinking. They are my rock and I am so proud to be a part of such an incredibly protective and devoted family. There is a quote by George Eliot that I read one time that describes my family perfectly. It says, "What greater thing is there for human souls than to feel that they are joined for life—to be with each other in silent unspeakable memories."

To my sweet Mckenna and Luke—you were the most important things in your Daddy's life. Even though he is gone, he lives through you every day, helping you in every way he possibly can. I wrote this book to you with every ounce of love that your Daddy and I have for you. He has influenced and is a part of each word written here. I am sure that he guided me in writing what we both want you to know. I cannot give you back your Daddy. If I could, I would in a heartbeat. But I can give you this. I can give you my memories. These memories are all I have. They are what shaped my life, they are what gave you yours. These memories *are* your Daddy's life, and you are his legacy. I hope you read these pages and learn about the man your Dad was, and the people he hopes you will be. I hope you learn something about him that you did not know and it makes you feel compelled to ask me questions—because you want to know more. The two of you have taught me more about hope and resilience than I could have ever known by myself, and for that alone I am proud to be your mother. I love you.

Finally, to Curtis—each day spent without you is a day spent wishing you were here. I look ahead to our family's future and know that there will be many memories we will need to create without you. Please know that even though you won't be here, you will be with us in our hearts. The first time Luke plays in a football game or when he graduates from high school, you will be in his heart. When Mckenna gets her driver's license or walks down the aisle, you will be with her in her heart. And while I watch them grow each day and guide them through their lives, you will be with me in my heart, too. We look forward to the day that we will meet you on the other side. Until then, we miss you and are thankful for the opportunity to have been blessed by having you in our lives. And as I have said before (not knowing it would be my last time), I now blow you a kiss and say *goodbye, my love*.

Curtis Alan Conner
November 8, 1975-July 31, 2008

Made in the USA
San Bernardino, CA
22 June 2013